Happiness...
all the way

Get the best out of life

Atul Sehgal

PUSTAK MAHAL®

Publishers
Pustak Mahal®

Administrative office and sale centre
J-3/16 , Daryaganj, New Delhi-110002
☎ 23276539, 23272783, 23272784 • *Fax:* 011-23260518
E-mail: info@pustakmahal.com • *Website:* www.pustakmahal.com

Branches
Bengaluru: ☎ 080-22234025 • *Telefax:* 080-22240209
E-mail: pustak@airtelmail.in • pustak@sancharnet.in
Mumbai: ☎ 022-22010941, 022-22053387
E-mail: rapidex@bom5.vsnl.net.in
Patna: ☎ 0612-3294193 • *Telefax:* 0612-2302719
E-mail: rapidexptn@rediffmail.com

ISBN 978-81-223-1406-9

Edition: 2014

Printed at : **Super Fine Book Binding Works, Tronica City (UP)**

Dedication

To the
memory of my mother
Late Smt. Pushpa Sehgal
It is all due to her

Contents

The Secret of Happiness

Ever since the dawn of human history, man has been in quest of happiness – always more and more of it. Through material accomplishments, mankind has all along sought only one thing in the ultimate analysis and that is happiness. Great adventures have been undertaken, battles have been fought, mammoth business ventures launched, hard spiritual penance performed and even rank criminal acts done – all for the attainment of this one ultimate objective. If we observe global history dating back to the authenticated period extending up to 3000 BC, we shall observe great civilizations come and perish; man, the common denominator of all civilizations and cultures has always been striving for happiness, which is only a distinct state of human mind. It is also in evidence that happiness has eluded a large chunk of mankind throughout the history of his existence.

Especially is this true of the present times when science and technology are making great strides. The irony of the present world is, that even after the invention of contrivances and devices for easier, smoother and convenient living, mental peace is at a premium. Man seeks happiness in greater wealth, better comforts but perhaps, gets obsessed with these material things and often lands himself in a vacuum where he feels suffocated and eventually gets frustrated.

The present times are the times of apparently great scientific progress. Man has made tremendous application of the available knowledge of science. Material progress has come, though the fruits of material progress do not seem to be equitably distributed among the global population. This is an irony of modern times, a contradiction of modern culture, which has brought prosperity alongside poverty, order along with chaos and peace co-existing with war among sections of human population dispersed across the globe.

Today we find a pauper and a billionaire equally unhappy and forlorn. Both seem to be running madly after something. That mirage makes them overactive, perhaps. Seeking happiness in material objects is a wild goose chase.

In modern occupational culture, work, per se, does not become an end in itself. The fruits of work are regarded the end and these are considered a right of human beings – for the great labour performed by them. 'Success brings happiness,' people say, but then success today depends on too many factors beyond the control of a person and if achieved, it can be regarded as a matter of chance, a fortuitous event. Thus hard, untiring efforts do not always guarantee success, which every man seeks and the degree of success in his endeavours determines the degree of his happiness. True happiness appears to have become a rare commodity; its definition and concept are misplaced and a large chunk of human population is seemingly living in a fool's paradise.

This work is an attempt to throw better light on the concept of true progress and true happiness. It is an honest endeavour to show in real perspective the secrets of peace and happiness which constitute human bliss. The writer would feel amply rewarded for his efforts if the matter presented in this work is rightly understood by the reader. No further expectations are there, for, the writer sincerely believes that right understanding would pave the way for right action, sooner or later. Man is the product of evolution and true knowledge is the foundation of the progress and evolution of man into the higher levels of consciousness.

ଔଷ

TRUE HAPPINESS

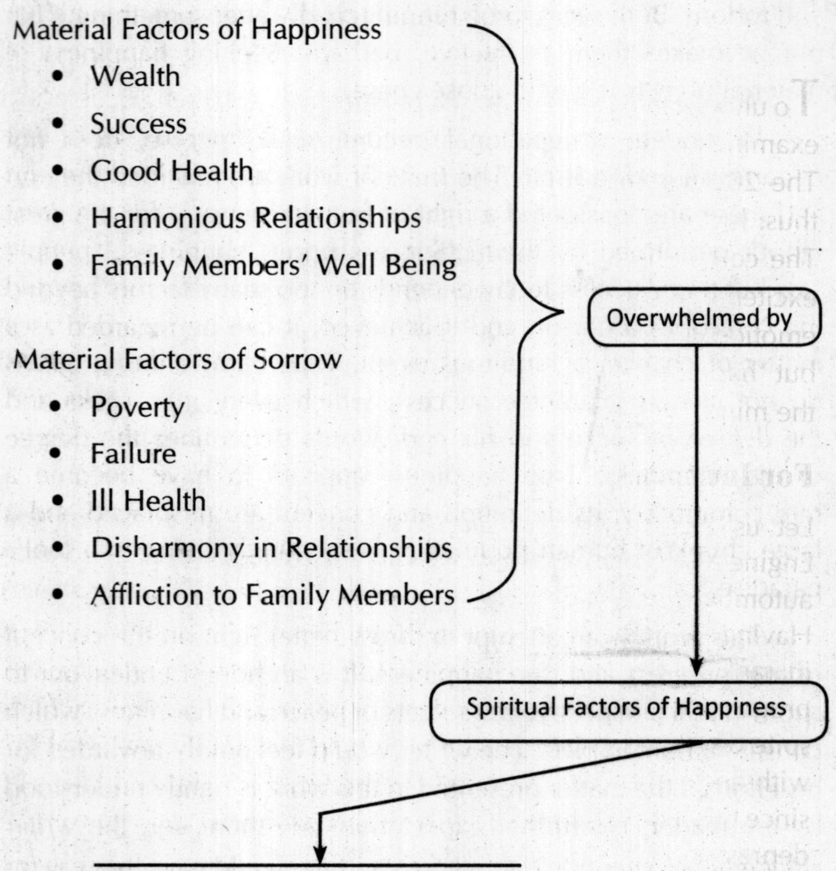

- Contentment
- Harmony with the Surroundings
- Reconciliation with the Circumstances
- Peace of Mind
- Vedic Regimen of Physical and Mental Healthcare

1. Defining Happiness

To understand a term in its true perspective, it is often necessary to examine its formal meaning, as recognized by literary authorities. The 20th century Chambers English Dictionary defines 'happy' thus: lucky, successful, possessing or enjoying pleasure or good. The commonly held notion about happiness is a state of joy or excitement in which the mind experiences some kind of positive emotion. The term 'pleasure' really goes with the physical senses, but 'happiness' is connected with the mind. It is clearly a state of the mind.

For Instance

Let us assume that you are a professional, say a Mechanical Engineer and working in a production company manufacturing automobile spare parts in the capacity of Production Manager. Having worked for five years, you were eligible for promotion in rank as General Manager as a part of the laid down career progression plan. But you think you were denied this promotion in spite of your eligibility and excellent performance and your peer, with an inferior record and less experience was promoted. Ever since this happened six months ago, you have grown unhappy and depressed. You are dejected and sad because you feel that you have not been given your due. You have a conscious belief that you are a more diligent and efficient professional than your peer. You also believe that your performance all through has been better than your peer's. But some machinations have worked against you, denying you what you deserve. This has started reflecting on your behaviour at home and outside. You have become irritable and moody. Clearly you are unhappy because your expectations were unfulfilled. You sought professional advancement but could

not make it — that is how an outsider might comment on you. Now pause and think for a while..... What kind of opinion have you been harbouring about your own self? Try to think critically or objectively without any self-bias. Are you having an exaggerated self image? Are you oblivious to your shortcomings? Do you have an inflated ego or an overwhelming self-pride?

Next, put yourself in the position of your company director who preferred to promote your colleague instead of you. Have you been really unfair and subjective in your preference? Have you allowed personal whims and fancies to prevail over objectivity? If the answer to former questions posed to your own self is a 'yes' and to those questions, when imagining yourself to be the company Director is a 'no', then clearly you are suffering from a false sense of self-glorification or a puffed-up ego. And this is really the cause of your unhappy state of mind. You are suffering from a grave illusion. This illusion is the cause of your troubles.

Dwelling upon this same hypothetical example, there is also a possibility that you may be ignorant of certain important facts and realities pertaining to your own capability as also your job performance, not to talk of capabilities and performance of your peer. Your Director is better placed to judge both of you on a comparative basis. It is said in an old proverb, "Do not judge yourself by what you think of yourself; rather judge yourself by what others think of you." Self-evaluation tends to be biased and subjective. There are very few persons who are capable of neat, critical assessment of their own self. Only the spiritually developed ones, who have risen above their pride, are capable of perfect self-assessment.

Of course, it does not mean that an ordinary person is incapable of it. It only goes to say that an ordinary person naturally tends to be erratic in evaluating his own self because he is blinded by ignorance. It is always possible for him to exercise the power of his intellect and think dispassionately for a certain while and if he did so, it is likely that he may get true answer to the seemingly vexing matter of the set of reasons behind his lack of success.

A Closer, Dispassionate View

Coming back to our example, we realize that you are unhappy because of your lack of professional success. But a closer, dispassionate view indicates that this promotion was really not deserved by you, which establishes pride as the first cause of unhappiness. Conversely, a lack of pride would result in happiness. Since vanity and pride are states of mind, happiness is also, clearly, a state of mind which is subject to the control of your intellect. It is just an emotion, like anger, sadness, excitement, resentment or delirium.

Consider another practical life situation now. Imagine yourself in the position of a trader in stocks and shares. You have had your shares of profits and losses under market fluctuations of past ten years but you have been able to draw out sufficient amounts of neat profits for your healthy sustenance and business operations. This time you made unprecedented, heavy investment in a particular stock in the expectation of a price boom. But contrary to all expert calculations, the market suffered a sharp crash and you were called upon to honour the financial commitments under investments. You incurred huge losses which wiped out your entire income of the previous year. You have just managed to survive and retain your fixed assets. This heavy financial setback has left you gloomy and depressed. Now what is the reason of this unhappiness?

It's not in Your Control

This was because of your 'bad luck', going again by the dictionary meaning of happiness. True, you are plagued by bad luck this time. But think; was avoidance of this loss within your control? You acted with great circumspection and after lots of professional calculations and yet suffered this loss. Indeed, it was beyond your control. If that be the case, then why should you be unhappy? Again, exercise your intellect and do some introspection. Yes, you felt that the money you lost was your possession. You are pained at its loss. But think again – Was the money truly yours? Had it truly belonged to you, it would have stayed with you on a permanent basis. You have not thrown it away in the gutter. You have also not gifted it away in charity. You have done nothing consciously and deliberately to dispossess it. But it went out of your hands and you watched helplessly. Realize the fact, that the cause of your unhappiness is attachment with something that was not really yours and appreciate that you are only the trustee of the money that you earned. You are subject to the inscrutable design of the Almighty who decides how long some possession should lie in your hand in your capacity as trustee. The moment you realize this deep truth, your mental depression would vanish. Once again, it is emphasized that happiness or the lack of it, is a state of mind determined by your notions.

It's Divine Control

Countless examples from real life can be cited in evidence of the fact that sadness, gloominess, despair, dejection, frustration etc. are all states of mind based on incorrect understanding or ignorance of the laws of cause and effect, of divine designs controlling mundane life and of metaphysical truths underlying phenomena of the universe. If you enlighten yourself on the real truths of life, you will always remain happy.

Let us go back to the dictionary definitions of the term 'happy'. You are normally expected to be happy if you are lucky, successful and possessed with worldly riches. But you can be happy even if you are unlucky, unsuccessful and dispossessed of a part of your wealth. You only have to see through worldly phenomena to discover the divine laws working behind them and realize the absolute truths which are immutable and eternal. Once you do that, you will acquire equanimity of mind.

ଔଷଠ

2. High Ambitions

Ambition is good as far as it motivates or propels you towards your charted goal. But sometimes, ambition can create more problems than the benefits it delivers. You may have seen highly ambitious persons going crazy, becoming neurotics. The great obsession with reward and result undermines quality of effort as nothing else can. Ambition transforming into greed can lead to delinquent behaviour. Indeed, greed knows no end. Having big ambitions is perfectly good, if you only regulate yourself at working honestly and diligently without worrying much about success. Success is the end result of a number of forces, many of which are not within your control. Remember that success is something like a final vector in vector-analysis, a subject studied under modern Physics. Whether considered over a plane or in absolute space, the summation of a number of vectors is always one single vector which has a specific magnitude and direction. Drawing an analogy from this, we represent the successful performance of a task or execution of a project in the following diagrammatic manner.

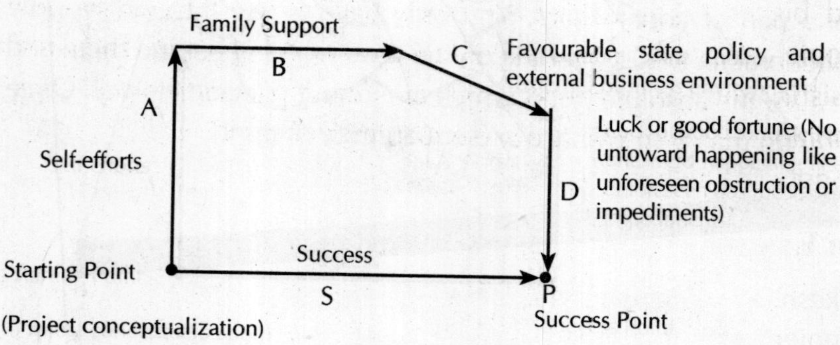

Explanation of the Diagram

In this example, a business venture is sought to be undertaken. For the successful accomplishment of this project, there are many governing factors. All these factors are represented by arrows A, B, C, D, and S. What these factors are – self-efforts, family support etc. is also mentioned alongside their vector (arrow) representations. Note that in the final analysis, the success vector S can be drawn only if the point P is reached by travelling the unique path along A,B,C and D. Success comes only when point P is reached. It can be appreciated that all the factors are crucial to success. Thus, mere self-efforts are not enough for success. If self-efforts are not enough, then why this constant obsession with success, especially when all other factors are simply beyond your control?

Rakesh was an Executive employed in a private company in New Delhi. He was ambitious in that he was keen to set up his own business and make a monthly earning of six digits in place of the five digits he was getting in his job. He gathered up his meagre savings and took the usual entrepreneurial risk by quitting his job and establishing a small manufacturing unit for electronic accessories. He faced initial teething troubles, but continued with patience and perseverance. His business began to pick up, gradually reaching breakeven after one year and he is doing well since that time.

This was a small story of success. There are many other bigger and bigger success stories in which people, highly ambitious people, have risen from rags to riches. Ambition is the common basis in all these entrepreneurial ventures. Persons, who are not ambitious, stay happy and contented with what they have. They do not venture out, do not take great risks.

An Example

Rakesh was ambitious, enterprising and successful. But is he happier today than he was earlier when earning a modest salary

in a career of service? Not really! The reason is that he is as ambitious today as he was then. He looks up to higher turnover, diversification and expansion which are all hard to come by. Growing competition has markedly altered the business environment. We find here that happiness is not merely a ‘function’ of success. It is also a ‘function’ of or related to ambition. The more ambitious you are, the more restless you will get; your mental peace would suffer a jolt if you found your targets hard to achieve. This happens with most of us. So does it imply that we all should stop being ambitious? There are some important points that need elaboration and clarification here.

Realistic Ambition is Positive

Ambition for personal material progress is good if you are not overly bothered about success. It is true that ambition sets the stage for certain achievements or accomplishments but then if you make the end more important than the means, you are in for trouble. Sooner than later, you are bound to land in a messy situation. You must realize that it is the means that are important and not the end. The end is like a deadpan object, a point fixed and left at that. It is something like a projection – real or imaginary, which is sought to be achieved. But a mental obsession with the end would imply that means for achieving the end shall not be given great importance. In the process, there is a great possibility of bypassing the laws of the land, of moral transgression.

Ambition is good as long as it is realistic; it is good as long as your acts are righteous and moral, as long as you do not damage the interests of others. Any efforts done in disregard of established laws of the land and of moral considerations would leave only adverse effects for peace and happiness. Remember that man is a spiritual being. His actions have wide repercussions not only on the corporeal body but also the mind, the intellect and the soul. The influences on the soul are impressions in the nature of indentations and have far-reaching consequences. They affect, in turn, the mind and the body. Action done in disregard of ethics is bound to adversely hit you back or bounce back at you. And before it actually bounces back, such action will, for sure, disturb your peace of mind. The adverse fallout will further aggravate this disturbed state.

Look at World History

World history is replete with the adventures of conquerors. They set sail in search of 'gold' in other countries, undertook hazardous journeys in sea-ships over thousands of miles and then fought tough battles in alien countries at great risk to their own lives. Ancient conquerors like Muhammad Ghori, Mahmud Ghazni and Alexander the great invaded the Indian subcontinent for the same purpose. During medieval times, Napoleon Bonaparte, Vasco-da-Gama etc. exemplified such conquerors. They were all motivated by ambition of acquiring riches or power by subjugating alien kingdoms. Ambition is conducive to peace of mind and happiness only if it helps the cause of humanity at large. Self-aggrandizement at the cost of others can never make anyone happy. This is a great, divine truth which must be understood by all those who seek to make their lives better and more worthwhile in this world. In fact, ambition can become a perversion too. In modern times, the lives of Hitler and Mussolini are the classic examples of ambition becoming a perversion. These persons gave in to their crazy, idiosyncratic ambitions and indulged in near barbarous acts. They persecuted the innocent and inflicted untold atrocities on people. Hitler willy-nilly landed himself in a situation that he had to commit suicide to save his own face. Ambition was the cause of all this.

What actually is behind perverted ambition? There are two fundamental evils stated to be the cause of perverted ambition. These are **greed** and **pride**. See that ambition per-se is not bad. But when **greed** and **pride** work up this ambition, they make it morbid. The resulting actions are imprudent and reckless which destroy harmony and happiness.

Unhealthy Ambition

In today's world too, some people perceive unhealthy ambition at not only individual level, but also at collective, institutional level. In the areas of business and trade, unethical practices are frequently observed through hypocritical behaviour at corporate and institutional levels. Bigger entities bullying or exploiting smaller entities is a manifestation of morbid ambition. Whether overt or covert, such actions are hardly conducive to peace and harmony of the entire set of population.

Pursuit of Achievable Goals

Ambition is a good servant but a bad master. So figure out what you want as well as how much is practically achievable given your resources and constraints and without trampling upon the interests of your brethren. Pursuit of goals fixed on such considerations alone shall give you peace of mind and happiness. Try to prudently crystallize your ambition rather than being driven by it. Fix up your targets and start concentrating on your efforts. If you worry too much about your goals and targets, you will not be able to properly concentrate on your efforts. The result will be – failure! Even modern management science teaches us that goals have to be fixed after weighing all pros and cons. Modern management techniques incorporate a SWOT analysis for business enterprises venturing into new areas. SWOT stands for Strengths – Weaknesses – Opportunities – Threats. This SWOT analysis is carried out for the purpose of identifying the company's strength and weakness areas having regard to its resources and limitations. The perceived opportunities and threats coming from the competitive business environment also are identified. After identifying all these aspects, a specific target is set.

Drawing analogy from the above SWOT analysis for a business enterprise, fix your short term, medium term and long term goals judiciously and then set about achieving them. Never forget that there are always uncertainties in successful completion of every activity because of factors beyond your control. So do not be disturbed by the thoughts of dangers from unknown, unexpected quarters. If you give in to such thoughts, it would be the surest way to spoil your peace of mind.

Realistic Targets are needed

In the matter of ambition, it needs to be emphasized that you should not bite more than you can chew. Cut your coat according to your cloth. Set your targets realistically and imaginatively. It is better to set smaller, achievable targets rather than high targets which drain up your resources and yet elude success. A hypothetical example from the Indian context would adequately illustrate this. A company named Mahesh Overseas was floated by a small time professional Mr. Mahesh Kumar for manufacturing footwear parts for export in partnership with an already established small scale businessperson. The said Mahesh Kumar was too ambitious a person to stay contented with petty achievements. Although his share of partnership was a minority share, he put his heart and soul in the venture. Fortunately, when they set up the venture, the external business environment was extremely favourable and conducive to growth of leather product export industry. The business turnover began multiplying. From a meagre turnover of ₹ 1 crore, it jumped to ₹ 50 crore within a period of just four years. Overawed by the unexpected success of his venture, Mahesh Kumar set his sights at much higher target and set up an ambitious expansion plan. Fortunately for him, the Government had, around that time, announced a policy of economic liberalization and garnering extra funds through the share market had been rendered easy. By expanding the equity base of the company through a rights issue, the entire money was smoothly raised. The required capacity expansion was successfully done. But it would have taken at least two years to show the result of the capacity expansion. Mahesh Kumar had become impatient and impetuous after his stupendous success in such a short time.

He desired to exploit the liberal business environment to his best advantage. He wanted to raise big funds for his two diversification projects. However, because of the fact that his flagship company Mahesh Overseas was yet to generate profits commensurate with the capacity expansion done, the financial institutions did not lend much finances. Mahesh Kumar, the hard-boiled businessman that he was, stayed undeterred. He decided to go back to the share market. Raising such huge funds was not going to be easy on the basis of the performance of his company, Mahesh Overseas. But as many others were doing, it was possible to manipulate the market price of the share of Mahesh Overseas company through stock-lot purchases.

This artificial jacking up of company's share price was an illegal practice which was being followed with impunity by many companies. '*When everybody is doing it, there is nothing wrong in it*', so thought Mahesh Kumar, quite aware of the weakness of the system in which business houses were violating the laws of the land, fleecing the innocent small investors and getting away with it. A strong nexus between governmental regulatory authority officials, companies and stock brokers was stated to be the reason behind this. Mahesh Kumar went ahead and made his devious plan. In this plan, the price of the shares of his company trading at ₹ 100 was to be jacked up to ₹ 290, simply by bulk purchase or 'hoarding' and then rights cum public issue at a fat premium would be floated. Shares were planned to be issued to the gullible, unsuspecting public at this high rate to raise the requisite funds. But unfortunately for Mahesh Kumar, somebody in the government suddenly woke up and foiled his plan. The public issue failed and the price of his company's share crashed to ₹ 16. Mahesh Kumar was jailed for blatant violation of existing laws and for defrauding the public. Shattered by prosecution and infamy, Mahesh Kumar disappeared into oblivion.

Don't Let Ambition Master You

The above is a typical example of what ambition can do if allowed to become your master. It can land you in marshy soils. It can blur your judgment and cloud your moral sense. When your judgment and moral sense are clouded, only disaster would be in store for you.

Therefore, understand that ambition is good to the extent that it makes way for your realistic growth without unduly straining and taxing your body and mind and without violating the laws of the land. The other important message that has come through is that you should always give greater priority to maintenance of physical and mental health at the optimum level. Stress and strain, mental and physical, rob life of the joy of living.

଄

ATTACHMENT

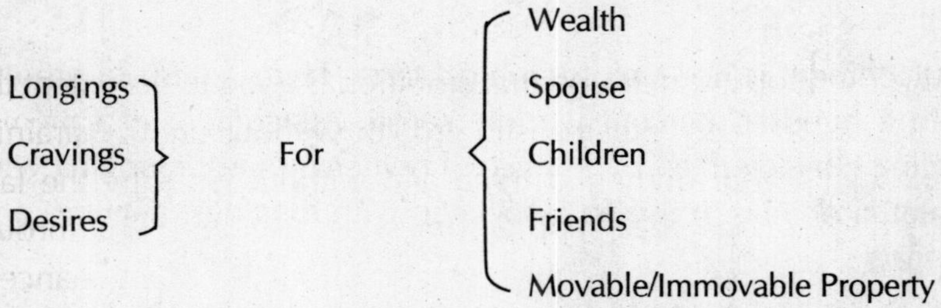

GENERATES

- Anxiety
- Worry
- Impatience
- Grief
- Frustration

REMEDY / CURE

- Understand the true nature of material possessions
- Understand the true purpose of human living
- Understand the true nature of human being

3. Attachment

Attachment is not a philosophical term. Here, I wish to present it in a hundred percent worldly sense. Attachment is a mental feeling characterized by a sense of ownership, of belonging with material objects. It is also associated with longings, cravings and desires.

Ashok is a school teacher, teaching middle level classes. Sometime ago, he suffered a cruel blow of fate when he lost his darling daughter, a school going child of twelve in a car accident. Four years have passed since that incident, but Ashok has not been able to recover from this shock. He has become unusually quiet, sees weird dreams at night and is unable to have a sound sleep. He suffers from frequent bouts of depression. A few months ago, he was advised by his friends to consult a professional psychiatrist. Ashok has had twelve sittings with the psychiatrist, but appears to be only marginally better. The psychiatrist has since kept him on tranquillizers for inducing sleep. But Ashok is hardly his former, cheerful self. Ironically Ashok's wife, who is equally afflicted by the tragedy, is quite normal. She appears calm, composed and regularly attends her office while doing full justice to all domestic chores. Why this difference between the husband and the wife? Ruma, their daughter, was the apple of her eye as much as her husband's. The difference lies in individual personalities. The difference exists in rationality of thinking, in a subtle understanding of the truths of everyday life phenomena, in degree of self-enlightenment.

Why do we grieve?

Think for a while – Why does a person grieve over the loss of a loved one? Why did Ashok grieve so much in the above example? He thought that Ruma was his daughter and her death was a personal loss to him. Was Ashok instrumental in her death or the cause of it? Indeed, it is a senseless or ridiculous question. It was just a quirk of fate and fate is nobody's mistress. Ashok's behaviour exemplifies attachment. Attachment is an illusory feeling of belongingness. We think that our children belong to us. We think we brought them into this world. But this is again an illusion. We are only instrumental in bringing them into the world. It is not much different from the perceived 'ownership' we often display with lifeless objects like house, car or jewellery. We are the agents, the instruments of the Almighty God in buying these lifeless objects or in bringing our children into this world. Everything belongs to Him. He is the supreme Owner.

We are only temporary custodians of all these objects which we regard our own. There is always His divine intelligence working behind phenomena which take away these objects, material or living from our custody. Then why fret over their 'loss'? Sri Krishna, the legendary figure of Hindu mythology says in Bhagwadgita, "When you were ushered into this world, you were empty-handed, then why do you worry over your losses? Whatever you seemingly acquired came from the Almighty God and whatever you lost went back to the same Almighty God. So wise men never moan over the loss of their so called possessions." Attachment is, indeed, the basis of grief. No wonder, attachment has been denounced in Hindu scriptures in strong terms. Attachment itself does not have any basis– it springs from illusion; it is far removed from reality. Therefore the prudent do not bemoan the death of their kith and kin and much less the loss of their material possessions, the lifeless objects that money can buy.

Lack of Faith is a Negativity

There is nothing new that is being attempted to be told in the above lines. It is an ancient philosophy which has served as a beacon of light and hope to many dejected, ignorant and aggrieved persons for thousands of years. The only matter of surprise is that in spite of this divine knowledge being so handy and within easy access of every person, many persons display its ignorance in thought and action. Ignorance is the root cause of all misery but then there is more to misery than mere ignorance. There is a lack of faith – faith in the existence of an omnipresent, omnipotent and omniscient God who is ever sympathetic, ever benevolent towards His human subjects. Knowledge of the truth that attachment is an illusion and faith in the justice of God Almighty makes a person acquire fortitude of mind. He then does not rejoice in gain nor grieve in loss. He views both success and failure alike. He keeps his balance and equanimity of mind in situations of loss and gain.

Attachment has many dimensions. You may be strongly attached to your father, wife or son. You are driving a car you purchased seven years ago. The car has never given any major trouble and you have had smooth journeys in it. There is something in the car – its colour or its number, which you believe is lucky for you! You are not inclined to sell it even though it has become an obsolete model. You have attachment for this car. You would not like to dispossess it. You would like to drive it as long as it gives you trouble-free service. Then imagine that your employer has sanctioned a loan for enabling you to buy a new car. But the amount of the loan along with financial resources from other places is not sufficient to fully pay for the car. The only way out for you is to sell your present car. You finally decide to dispose of your present car and go ahead for the new one. You were not keen to dispossess it but circumstances made you do it. You were forced to act against your own wish. You thought that after say, another two years, the old car may become unserviceable because its spares may not be available, being an obsolete model. Further you also apprehend that the employer's loan facility available today may not be there for the asking in the future, if your employer company's fortune takes a downswing. It can be said that you have made a good, sensible, rational decision. You should be complimented for this, for, you have overcome extraneous thinking caused by attachment.

Another Example

Take another example. You are a habitual, regular player on the speculation market. You committed big stakes on gold, the yellow metal which your astrologer friend stated was lucky for you. Anticipating surge in price, you put huge stakes on a substantial amount of gold. But, the prices started taking a downslide and before you could fix up your mind on what to do, the loss on your speculation accumulated to one million dollars. You had either to square up the deal or carry it forward in the grim hope of prices firming up. You decided to square up the deal after consulting your brokers and market experts who indicated a global recessionary trend in the price. You were not unduly grieved because in the previous session you had made a profit of 750 thousand dollars on speculation of copper.

You were not much upset about the whole thing regarding it as a part of the game until after three weeks when you looked at the newspaper quotations of the price of gold. They had increased beyond everybody's expectations! The marketmen and speculators were taken aback! Another week later, the price stood at a level of twelve percent higher than the original transaction price. How did you feel? Shattered? Distraught? You felt so depressed over it as if you had lost your world and again the casualty was your mental peace which, arguably, is your dearest possession. This is another dimension of attachment – attachment with money which you thought was your own. Referring to the example of chapter 1, realize that the money lost was not your own. Nobody has snatched it from you. Nobody has stolen it. You entered into a deal in the best of your wisdom and the market forces, which were beyond your control, caused you the loss of money. If the

market forces are not in your control, then who controls them? Surely, in the 21st century, nobody is living in a country with lawlessness or anarchy. Your country has tough laws and stringent law enforcement because of which manipulators or fly-by-night operators cannot hijack the speculation market. So it was because of international economic factors, the usual demand and supply reasons. Hence, it stands to reason that the controller of the market is none other than the Almighty God. Remember, nothing in this world ever happens by chance. There is always a divine design behind every such gain or loss.

No Cause for Grief

In your case, you did not lose money because of your foolhardiness or carelessness. You played your cards well, but luck was not in your favour. You played your cards well because your buy and sell decisions were rational. The unexpected happened. Two conclusions emerge from this episode. First, the money was not lost because of your mistake. Secondly, the market phenomena are orchestrated by the supreme power, God who alone is the master of the world and all worldly objects. We human beings are only custodians of his wealth. Now, still do you think there is any cause for grief? Only a fool shall grieve in these circumstances.

Fallacious Belongingness

Attachment with brothers, sisters, parents, children, friends, and spouse also is a fallacious sense of belongingness. In practice, though, it is extremely difficult to defeat this feeling. Why is it so? Because we believe that these persons belong to us. In fact there is an element of selfishness behind this feeling. We receive some benefit, material or emotional, through our relationship with each of these persons. Our parents are ever ready to bail us out of troubled waters. They always shower that unique love for which we crave and long. The wife or husband is our partner in running the house, in domestic chores, in love. Our spouse is giving us something in all these areas. Is there not a vivid element of selfishness in our relationship with parents and spouse? Wherever there is selfishness, there is attachment. And wherever there is attachment there is misery. This fundamental truth must be clearly understood to realize what havoc attachment can wreak on our lives. Pursue your filial or conjugal relationships with a pure sense of duty without that element of selfishness. You will enjoy the relationship manifold. Moreover, you will be able to avoid stressful situations. You will be able to avoid strife, discord and all attendant troubles. Consider the alarming number of divorce cases filed in the courts of America and Europe. That gross feeling of attachment or of selfishness in relationship is the cause of marital misery.

Try to give rather than demand and you will find the entire horizon of mutual relationships change, change for the better. Your spouse affords you a sense of security and satisfies your craving for love. Attachment here has that clear element of selfishness which engenders misery. If you are selfish, you become conscious of your rights; you demand your rights. Even in the sacred institution of marriage and family, you start demanding conjugal and filial rights. Obsession with rights is the root cause of many troubles. What actually happens is that when you become demanding and in an attempt to obtain your rights, you become blind to others' limitations in satisfying your demands. You become oblivious to the helplessness of your husband or wife in meeting your demands. The result? Marital discord! Imagine how much stress, how much tension and how much strife can be avoided, if only people begin thinking in terms of delivering rather than demanding. It is as simple as it appears–the solution to problems of conjugal discord, divorce and all their attendant issues.

The Evil form of Attachment

What is the lesson to be learnt from the above? Try to give up the fundamentally fallacious feeling of attachment. But it also does not mean that living in this world you should become an ascetic by fully detaching yourself from everything. Far from it. Attachment in so far it is based on selfish instinct should be shed. Attachment in so far it is based on a false, misplaced notion of ownership should be shed. And mind you, this is not difficult to do. A proper mix of enlightenment (or understanding), willpower and patience is all that it will take to bring these simple pieces of advice into effect.

Attachment as an evil has been denounced in no uncertain terms by the ancient Hindu sages endowed with great, almost divine wisdom. The Vedas, Upanishads and *Bhagwadgita* contain many stanzas where the evil of attachment has been condemned. Some readers might be led into drawing a naive inference from this that all this sermonizing has got a purely religious character. What has it to do with the material world of men, money and machines? This message is as relevant to material life as it is to spiritual life. Therefore, for peace, progress and prosperity, try to break off the stranglehold of attachment on your mind. Peace, progress and prosperity can come only with harmony and harmony can be maintained only by assiduous adherence to the philosophy of 'Karmayog' enshrined in *Bhagwadgita* and by a continuous and conscious attempt to overcome the evils of *kaam* (desire) *krodh* (anger), *lobh* (greed), *moh* (attachment) and *mad* (pride).

In Contemporary Living

Before bringing this small humble exposition of the evil of attachment to a close, it would be necessary to touch upon another dimension of attachment in the context of contemporary living. And that is – attachment with comforts. Is it not true? Thanks to the progress of science and technology, the various implements for making human living comfortable have become popular, rather commonplace. A large number of such implements and devices are part and parcel of our homes and places of work. We have become so much comfort-seeking, that we are unable to do without air conditioners, sleek Toyotas and BMWs and a host of other labour saving or weather conditioning devices. We must use them to the extent they are necessary for our professional life. But too much dependence on them merely for the sake of individual comfort carries damaging effects on health, both physical and mental. It might appear strange that these things can affect mental health. But it is, nevertheless, true because body and mind cannot be considered separately in the matter of health and disease.

Drawing upon the classical medical philosophy of Aayurved, any irritant that affects the body can also affect the mind and any adverse stimulus for the mind can leave a bad effect on the body. Therefore, use comfort providing devices to the extent they are needed for professional work or maintaining optimum health, but do not develop attachment with them. Attachment will result in overuse – rather abuse which will bring detrimental effects. This exactly is the reason why Yoga, the regimen for improving the physical, mental and spiritual faculties of man, strongly emphasizes on restriction of human comforts. Yoga is tremendously gaining in popularity all over the world as an effective means of stress alleviation.

ଔଔ

ANGER

CAUSES OF ANGER

- Injured Ego
- Belied Expectations
- Internal Frustration

EFFECTS OF ANGER

- Loss of Esteem
- Erosion of Mental Peace
- Bad Effect on Health
- Strain in Relationships

CURE OF ANGER

- Water Down the Ego
- Have Realistic Expectations
- Better Understanding of Nature of Self and Others
- Healthy Lifestyle Including Diet

4. Anger

This chapter treats the subject of anger — the emotional impulse which is a natural ingredient of human behaviour and which is the bane of human relationships. Anger is perfectly natural to most persons in odd situations. Why do we get angry? Are anger and the behaviour that it generates beneficial? Is it possible to suppress and control it? Is it always advisable that anger should be controlled? What does anger do to our physiological system? The answers to many of these questions are generally known to people at large. But there is more to these answers than the common belief. What is being conveyed in these lines is that anger causes a host of problems but perhaps solves very few – this is the common belief. Anger is regarded just as another emotion like excitement, anxiety or happiness. But this term has a much wider canvas. Hindu scriptures regard anger as another cardinal evil which generates many other evils. Anger generates bitterness and animosity; it often leads to physical violence as well.

It is not my intention to delve into the details of this subject from the point of view of psychology or behavioural sciences. Far from it, I only intend to focus on the role played by the human frailty known as anger in undermining happiness and mental peace of human beings. And with examples from day to day life of human mortals, an attempt shall be made to show in clear, proper light why we all should try to curb anger if we desire real happiness and peace. Remember, neither true happiness nor peace of mind can be procured through wealth. There are people who are happy in spite of their poverty and there are others who are unhappy in spite of all their great riches. The kaleidoscopic beauty of human life is manifest in a wonderfully great variety and shades of nature, temperament, behaviour, attitude, belief and moral character. The intelligent person would try to understand that behind all apparent perversities of human behaviour there is a working of beliefs and attitudes. And these beliefs and attitudes spring from culture. Where does culture come from? It has divine sources but its manifestations are very much material, mundane.

An Example

Rita is a middle-aged lady with two teenaged children. Professionally qualified and well-employed as a school teacher, she leads a hyperactive life attending to the twin responsibilities of job and home. At home, she attends to the domestic chores of cooking and overall upkeep. Her duties are, in fact, more arduous than her husband's who does not attend to any domestic chores. Like a typical, modern working but innately traditional Indian housewife, she painstakingly tries to do full justice to her job outside and duties at home. The routine is quite tiring and taxing and leaves her thoroughly exhausted at the end of the day. But the routine has also been telling upon her mood and general temperament. She has become irritable and short-tempered. At the slightest provocation, she becomes angry and, if argued with, often bursts into a flood of rage. She is, in fact, sore at her husband Ravi, who ought to be helping her at her domestic chores, but doesn't care to do it like a typical, pampered Indian male. Rita loses her temper over petty matters. At school, the children of her class have given her the epithet of 'witch'. What have the repeated bouts of anger done to her?

Her blood pressure remains morbidly high. Her attending physician has advised her to remain on anti-hypertensive drugs. Her overall physical health has certainly gone down. She was also advised to maintain a calm and relaxed mental disposition. But she finds rather difficult to do it. Her repressed feeling of helplessness against her indifferent and irresponsible husband comes out in the form of repeated bouts of anger. Here it would be important to point out what colossal damage anger can do to your system. It was estimated some years ago that fifteen minutes of angry disposition is enough to sap a person's energy to perform eight hours of constructive work. Anger is a great enemy of your health, stamina and vitality. It saps your creative energy as nothing else does. It is a much, much greater evil than most of the people believe or imagine. The great, ancient Indian medical science of Aayurved regards anger as an important cause in the vitiation of '*vaat*', one of the three basic body humours. And vitiation of *vaat* is the prime factor in the development of any disease process in the body. Anger veritably takes you to the mouth of hell.

Control Your Temper

In the example under discussion, the lady Rita found her physical and mental health deteriorating with the doctors unable to correct her condition except putting her on regular dose of anti hypertensive drugs. She was advised to change her lifestyle, which was found to be quite stressful. But purely acting on her own, she found it extremely difficult to change things. A few sessions with a psychotherapist also followed. She was suggested to change her attitude towards things, to stop taking things too seriously and control her temper. Ever since she has made deliberate attempts at controlling her temper, she has found a sea change in persons around her, even in her husband! People interacting with her have grown more co-operative, sympathetic and friendly. In fact, Rita has come to have a different aura altogether. She now exudes cheer and this behaviour has helped to make her life smoother and more comfortable. Stress appears to have been controlled and alleviated, quite successfully. The basic poison in the life of Rita was nothing but anger. This one evil, when allowed to have its way, produced a multitude of problems and rendered life burdensome and miserable. But when this evil is vanquished, life becomes enjoyable and meaningful once again. It is said that 'you live only once and if you live well, once is enough!' Control of anger is immeasurably beneficial.

Why do you succumb to that instantaneous fit of rage? When somebody hurls insults at you, when persons do not measure up to your expectations in their work or dealings with you – these are the situations when anger takes the hold of you. But think for a while, of what use is anger? It precipitates violent situations, often leading to brawls of sorts. It snaps relationships in the twinkling of an eye; it creates sworn enemies out of bosom friends; it is anathema to construction, co-operation and success.

Another Example

Imagine yourself in the position of a top level executive of a multi-billion dollar company. In your top managerial role, you are not called upon to do any work directly; you only have to supervise the work of others. You are provided with full powers to hire, fire, punish and reward. Modern management theories have described different types of managerial behaviour. Each one has merits and demerits. You, by nature, are short-tempered. You cannot tolerate truancy and indiscipline in your juniors. You tend to scold them left and right wherever they work in an indifferent manner or violate office discipline. You are almost a terror for your subordinates. Imagine that you are a habitual 'fire-spitting' boss. You show your unhappiness in loud, explicit terms by scolding and shouting at your juniors whenever they commit mistakes.

You may never have thought in terms of milder way of dealing with your subordinates. But if you just ponder over this for a while, you would realize that if you made your behaviour with your juniors mild and polite, both stand to gain! This is because the power to hire, fire, reward and punish the juniors vests entirely in you. There is nothing you are going to gain through angry behaviour except the silly satisfaction of your ego. On the other hand, more humane and polite behaviour is not going to demotivate your juniors in their work. Rather they will be encouraged to discuss with you their problems, some of which could be genuine and workable solutions could be found out. Even if they do not have any circumstantial problems, they will try to improve upon their performance and overcome their weaknesses. And you, on your part, shall be spared of all the deleterious effects of anger on the mind and body. The damaging effect of anger may not be immediately manifest. It may just show up years later in the form of high blood pressure or duodenal ulcer or stroke.

Anger is not Uncontrollable

Anger is a great poison in human relationships – formal or informal, official or unofficial. It just cuts off harmonious vibrations between two individuals and creates conditions conducive to hatred, enmity and bitterness. You think, that it is perfectly natural to get angry; you feel that it is such a spontaneous outburst of emotion that to suggest control over anger is to suggest changing your own nature. "Nature is nobody's servant," you might argue and observe that everybody is controlled by his or her nature. "Nature is something one is born with. It is extremely difficult to change your nature. Any sermon or talk exhorting us to change the nature is glib talk – it is unrealistic," you may further argue.

To answer the above questions, it would be necessary to go into the basic fundamentals of human nature. What constitutes human nature? Why does a man behave the way he does? Why does another man display a different behaviour? Remember, man is his corporeal body, subtle body and soul – all intertwined. The mind which is part of the subtle body is the seat of all emotions. The intellect, which is another element of the subtle body, is our faculty through which we do cognitive learning and exercise discrimination between right and the wrong, between truth and untruth. The subtle body is that part of the human being which consists of mind, intellect and ego. The soul is the subtle divine element in man which is primordial, eternal and indestructible.

Na Jaayte Mriyate Vaa kadaachinnaayam
Bhootvaa Bhavitaa Vaa Na Bhooyah
Ajo Nityah Shaashvatoyam Puraano
Na Hanyate Hanyamaane Shareeray !!

(The soul is unborn, eternal, everlasting and primeval; even though the body is slain, the soul is not.)

(Shrimad Bhagwadgita, Chapter#2, Shlok#20)

According to Aayurved

In the light of the above definitions, it would be proper to say that human nature is determined by the corporeal body and the subtle body. First, human nature is determined by the type of physical constitution that a person has been born with. This is called *prakriti* in Aayurved, the oriental science of human life. There are seven types of *prakriti*. The entire human population can be divided into seven *prakriti*-types. There are some specific, gross, physical and mental traits peculiar to a *prakriti*-type. A person may be calm, quiet and of mild temper. Another may be restless and irritable. Yet another may have an extremely short temper and fiery disposition. All this is, understandably, because of mind and the factors influencing it. But the mind itself is subject to the influence of other elements, internal or external to the human organism. The internal elements are the intellect and the soul. The intellect has the great power to discriminate between the right and the wrong, between the real and the deceptive. It is indeed this intellect which makes man a superior being among God's creations. But the intellect does not possess a spiritual character. It is also subject to banal influences but it can be put in the right functional mode through material conditioning and above all, through spiritual power.

Making use of your intellect, your thinking, comprehending and analyzing ability, realize the uselessness of anger and try to control it. Do not give in to it; try to become the master of it. Anger benumbs your intellectual reasoning and makes you a virtual monster for the period it is in control. So never let anger control you.

Anger is Futile

Sometimes you get angry at your wife because she has not cooked your meal properly – your snack has too little salt or too much spice in it or your favourite dish, pizza has not been baked properly.

I have heard of husbands who throw away their dining plate in a fit of anger. Especially is this the case in many households in India, where the wife is traditionally subdued and has to stand husband's tantrums. What does the husband gain by bursting into that rage? Nothing! In fact if you are one of those husbands, you surely would be ruing your act after every episode of anger. Such behaviour creates marital disharmony and discord. In western societies, this often becomes an easy base for obtaining divorce. In almost all situations of angry behaviour, a person usually realizes the futility of his action sooner than later, after the act. He repents his behaviour, for, it often leaves scars in relationships. Today global life has become quite complex. You cannot do anything in isolation. In every institution, you have to work co-operatively. Only then can you have a smooth sailing in all activities of your life. But angry behaviour is bound to isolate you from your kith and kin, peers, juniors or subordinates at work or anybody else you interact with. Anger is the great enemy of success and material progress. You must eschew it.

Do you think the above is all plain theoretical sermonizing? Read through it once again and you would appreciate how close it is to reality, to your practical life. You would simply be surprised at the enormous gain in practical and material terms that is bound to accrue to you if only you vanquished your anger.

Is it Possible to Control Anger?

But you may ask "What if somebody belittles me, insults me or even abuses me? Is it possible to control anger or rather is it desirable to control anger in such situations?" Human vanity or self-respect is an important element of man's personality. If somebody hurts your self-respect or encroaches on your self-dignity, sharp reaction in retaliation is likely and natural. Do react by all means but without giving in to that surge of rage. Consciously try to condition yourself that in all such situations, you will not lose your temper. Try to redeem your prestige through words or gestures without the element of anger in it. It is possible and it works better in redeeming your hurt prestige and in defusing tension of the situation as well. Respond rather than react. If faced with extremely rude behaviour calling for retribution, kill your tormentor with kindness. No, never think that this is a sign of cowardice. In fact, on the contrary, it is a sign of audacity and of steadfastness of mind. What is the advantage in this kind of behaviour? In ninety percent of cases, it will make your tormentor feel apologetic for his behaviour. He will feel more anguished. He may even think he committed a great blunder. There may, in the ultimate analysis, be no damage done to relationship between you and him. On the other hand misunderstandings may be removed. A new consensus may be created and a whiff of fresh air may begin to flow in your relationship. Try to experiment and experience this once and you will realize the futility, nay poisonous intensity of anger and its destructive role in human relationships and in undermining all other constructive activities based on these relationships.

This discussion can hardly be considered as complete, if the positive role of anger in human life is not touched upon. In some situations, anger indeed plays a positive, beneficial and constructive role. For dealing with enemy on the battlefield or with criminals as a state police person, anger is a constructive element of behaviour, as it helps you to perform your solemn duty effectively. In another situation, dealing with your wayward child may require angry behaviour. In all these situations, anger is constructive because it helps you to perform your duties in a proper and effective manner. In the ultimate analysis, it needs to be made clear that anger is born out of ignorance and delusion. Anger is identified by its external manifestations – derisive speech and violent action. But, more often than not, even if external manifestations are not visible, anger lurks in the mind. It is in the mind that anger has to be destroyed. For this, positive conditioning of mind through determination, lifestyle correction and spiritual practice are needed. These are dealt with at length in chapter 15 of this book.

THE DOCTRINE OF KARMA

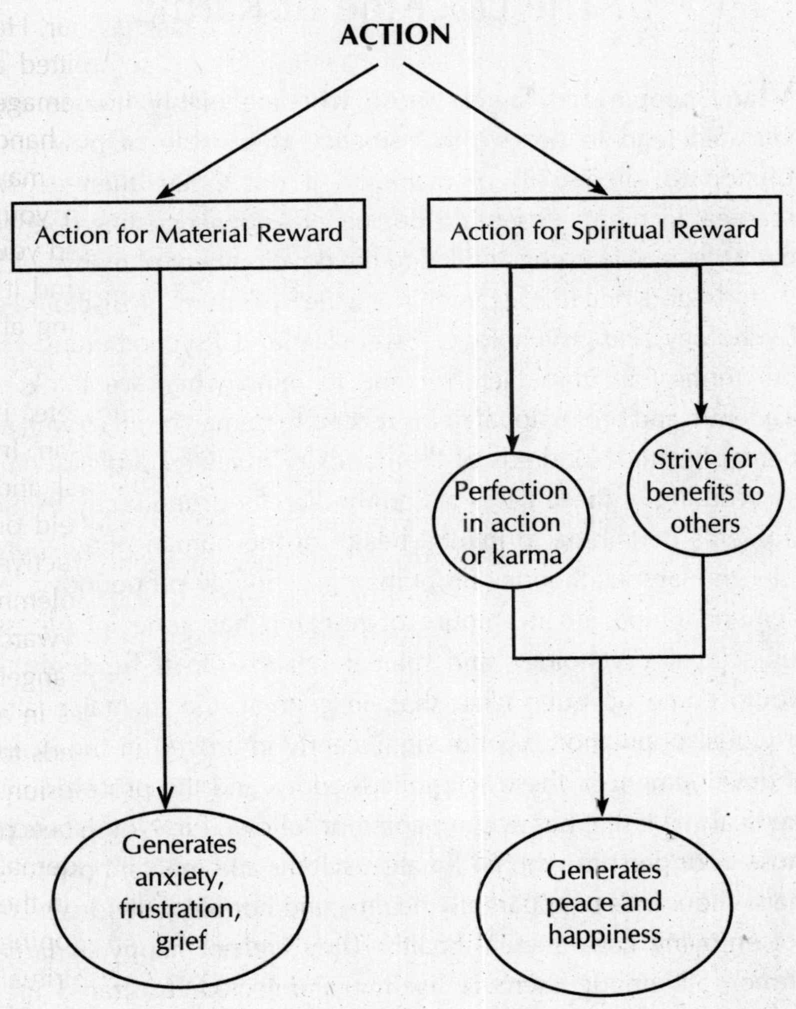

5. The Doctrine of Karma

Many people and largely those who are highly literate and educated tend to believe that science is capable of providing solution to all the ills of mankind, if not today, then in the foreseeable future. Scientific pursuit of knowledge has opened many vistas of learning and led to the development of many fields of study and practice, covering a wide spectrum of disciplines. Psychology, Parapsychology, Psychiatry and Psychotherapy are four terms that immediately come to mind when we think of academic and professional fields related to human mind as well as mental health. Hundreds of thousands of qualified professionals are working in these fields attending directly or indirectly to the problems pertaining to mental health of the human population. After the famous theories on human psychology propounded by Sigmund Freud, great amount of research has gone into these subjects of psychology and mental health. On a hindsight it would come up quite clear that, in general, the mental health of global population has not significantly improved in the wake of development of these scientific theories and the professional, medical work that has accompanied or followed it. Not to talk of those poor persons who fill lunatic asylums and mental hospitals, many thousands of apparently healthy and normal individuals are not enjoying good mental health. They are not happy. A large proportion among them is leading a dejected, frustrated life. These persons are depressed and many of them have to depend regularly on tranquillizers, alcohol or sleeping pills. Anxiety is mental state peculiar to many persons. Anxiety is frequently the result of attachment with the result of your efforts in any activity. It is the offshoot of your obsession with success. The morbid mental state of depression is the result of failure, setback in life. You set up ambitious targets, employ your resources and work hard at the project. But success eludes you. You are unable to stand failure and pass off into a state of mental depression.

Why do we Succumb to Silly Emotions?

We all know the utter uselessness of worry, anxiety and grief. Yet we succumb to such emotions. Auto suggestion, a prescription of modern psychiatry, is something that patients find difficult to bring into practice. What is the reason that such types of prescription are not practicable? Why do they remain pieces of advice on paper with a character which is largely theoretical? The answer to these questions is that the real nature of human organism is not understood. What afflicts the mind and how is not truly recognized. The banal forces that influence the mind still remain shrouded in mystery. Whereas the modern scientists know quite a lot about the human body and its morbid conditions, they know very little about mind, mental phenomena like memory as well as perception and about mental illness. Science may yet take hundreds of years to fathom mental and spiritual phenomena.

Fortunately, however, much of the knowledge pertaining to mind and the spirit is available in the divine, primordial scriptures – the Vedas and Upanishads. But most of us are not tapping this knowledge. Why? The probable reason is that today our intellects lie benumbed. There is a crisis of faith prevailing all around. We have become skeptic and narrow-visioned. Our intellectual process is governed by our preconceived notions, prejudices and idiosyncrasies. In spite of all the professional academic degrees and diplomas, in spite of the great amount of empirical knowledge of worldly affairs stored as 'bits' in the memory chips of computers and in spite of all the knowledge of mundane affairs that we profess to have, we are often unable to discriminate between truth and untruth, between right and wrong, between illusion and reality and between fact and fiction. This explains why the global population is still groping in the dark despite a fund of true knowledge of mental phenomena and spiritual matters being available in our ancient scriptures.

Gita's Philosophy

Talking in the context of human happiness, the divine law of *karma* enunciated in Bhagwadgita needs to be elaborately discussed here. We have to shed our preconceived notions while picking out the pearls of wisdom from our scriptures. With an open mind, if we try to understand the import of the doctrine of *karma*, we shall realize that it is indeed the door to true freedom of mind – freedom from attachment and from anxiety about success or failure of our effort. It is only in this freedom, that divine happiness and bliss can be attained.

Dozens of treatises and commentaries have been written on Bhagwadgita by learned individuals. Almost each one has extolled the divine wisdom contained in the law of *karma*. As you sow, so shall you reap. Every action has equal but opposite reaction. If you work, you are bound to get the reward. But the time and the form of this reward and also the manner of its bestowal is not in your own hands. It is in the hand of the master of the universe, the Almighty God. I have repeatedly emphasized on the importance of faith, open mindedness and of shedding prejudice because without these, the true comprehension of the law of *karma* cannot be made by the ordinary human mortal. The agnostic lives in his own narrow world. Divine truths can only be understood by that person who is having faith in the existence of an almighty, all pervading super entity called God. Faith develops easily in a medium of open-mindedness and logical thinking. If a person says he doesn't believe in God because he is a rationalist, that person certainly does not understand the meaning of rationality. For, to the true rationalist the existence of God becomes immediately manifest.

Efforts are Never in Vain

Therefore, rest assured that reward will accrue to you for your efforts and shall be truly commensurate with the efforts. Do not worry over the uncertain happening – the stroke of misfortune which may deprive you of success. If you do not attain success when expected, do not fret. Reward shall come to you in some other form, at some other time, which He considers appropriate. Leave the result of your efforts to God. Once you focus your energies on tasks in hand and proper accomplishment of the same, your attachment with reward or obsession with result shall automatically diminish. It is a very practical matter. The principle of duty without attachment has to be practically followed for that feeling of satisfaction and of joy. Once you experience this feeling, you will realize the utter uselessness of attachment. In fact you should get so engrossed in your duty or work that you begin to enjoy it. Try to improve upon your manners and methods of work. Strive to attain perfection in your task-performance. This is a rigorous action plan. But actual improvement will come with practice. The more you are able to improve upon your performance and the utilization of your time and other resources, the more detached you will grow with the reward of your tasks. The more detached you become, you will grow yet more active and energetic in working proficiently. In the process, do not give in to lethargy and distractions. Try to achieve better concentration, try to optimally utilize your time and you will be able to achieve a lot. This achievement is something like a 'credit' entry in your ledger maintained by God. He will give you your due as and when and in the manner, He deems appropriate. But you cannot encash this credit at will. Understand this great truth and you will be easily able to make your life productive and happy at the same time. You will be able to rid yourself of tension and stress. More than that, you will be able to have a feel of the higher consciousness through which one attains the state of divine bliss.

Each one of us has some fixed goals or targets in mind, some short term and others long term, in our various fields of endeavour. Just sit back and think one evening — how much time you actually spend in a day working in pursuit of your goals, how much time you spend in idle gossip, how much time is lost in brooding over past events and how much is lost worrying about your future. You would be surprised to find that considerable time and energy is wasted in fretting over the past and worrying about the future. How many of us optimally use our present? Live for the present, not in the past, nor in the future. How you make use of your present is going to determine your future. The past is anyway buried under the sands of time.

Law of Karma as Understood

There are some among the modern intellectuals and contemporary thinkers who offer a slightly different explanation of the law of *karma*. They say that if you are obsessed with the result of your *karma* or action, you are a prisoner of your past. If you cease to be a prisoner of your past, you are in the realm of freedom – freedom to act and freedom to achieve. They say that if you arrive in this realm of freedom you can achieve anything through the dint of your efforts. You can reach the skies and go for the stars.

This kind of philosophy is good for providing superficial relief to the ambitious, tension ridden individual of today. But does it not skirt the truth? The truth is that we are always free to act. Whether or not we suffer from a hangover of our past, we have full freedom to act the way we like. And to all our actions, there will be reaction – reactions of reward. But reward will come from the Almighty God. This is His domain. Our domain is the domain of action. His domain is that of reward. We cannot interfere in

His work. Remember, He also does not interfere in our work. Our minds are frail; they succumb to greed, to attachment, to lust, to desire. But our intellect is always there to check the errant mind. Intellect has that great power of discriminating between good and bad action.

An Instance

Mr. James is a qualified technician. He was well employed in a medium sized production company. Unfortunately, a recessionary trend set in the industry and the company had to lay off many of its employees. Mr. James was one of those retrenched. He has been running from pillar to post over six months trying to get a new job. So far, he has failed to secure a job. He must have sent in at least a hundred job applications during this period but has not been successful. He was quite hopeful, while trying hard. But continued failure has made him dejected and frustrated. He made vigorous efforts at job hunting for full five months. But over the last one month he has been overtaken by despair and dejection. His efforts have been in vain. He passes much time in idle brooding. If he continues this way for a long time, he might make a mental wreck of himself.

Fortunately Mr. James is living in a developed well-regulated country and gets an unemployment allowance, which is enough only to meet his basic necessities. He, however, is unable to meet many of his family expenses. What should he do? He should understand that he must go on trying without wasting time or opportunity. There should be no let up in his efforts. Let frustration, even if it sets in, not hamper his efforts. For, efforts are his duty. If, for some reason, you are not making proper efforts in the direction of your goal, you are under-performing your duty. This would naturally work to your detriment. In the above example, therefore, James should not be run down by despair, because the feeling of despair will stifle his efforts. If he does not perform his efforts at job-searching or embarking on any alternative means of livelihood properly, he would probably miss out on some positive opportunities and his chances of getting a job or establishing business would be diminished. Introspecting on reasons of failure, he has to continue his efforts and leave the result to the benevolent God. Trying times throw up rare opportunities of growth. He has to make efforts to identify and tap one of these opportunities. It is his efforts which will pay him later and will stand him in good stead in the future. With this kind of approach backed by the philosophy of *karma* without attachment, he is bound to emerge a winner – make no bones about it.

In practical life, there are innumerable instances of persons giving up their pursuit of goals after some modest efforts. In all these cases, there is a common denominator—obsession with success or the positive result of efforts. These persons are impatient; they are anxious about the reward of their efforts; they tend to give up or admit defeat easily. These people do not have the tenacity to try again and again. Naturally, success often eludes them. They blame it on their stars, on other persons or their circumstances but the fault really is their own. Luck or fortune, in any case, is a factor beyond the control of the performer. So the only important factor from the point of view of the performer is the work itself. He should regard his work as an oblation to God. If he did this, he would be free from the bondage of attachment, his mind would remain peaceful and he would be able to derive real joy out of his living. This is a major secret of meaningful living and of happiness.

Utility of the Doctrine of Karma

The doctrine of *karma* can be understood better through another simplified explanation. Make your work or duty as the end rather than a means to an end. It is good to have well-defined goals but goals should not be the end. It sounds a bit odd and paradoxical to say that you should not make your objective as your end. But the doctrine of *karma* says precisely this. When we do our work, the end becomes most important to us and everything else comes to occupy a secondary place. In the process, work performance actually suffers. And mind you, it is not easy to train your mind on this approach. But practice makes it possible. In our business organizations and commercial establishments today, we often demand result-oriented professionals. I dare say that business executives who are overly result-oriented rather than work oriented, tend to have a typically Machiavellian approach. They will try to achieve the result through any means. Sometimes, rather frequently, rules of propriety are thrown to the winds and even laws bypassed to beat the competition. This is not a healthy approach. In case, however, 'result-oriented' means oriented towards beneficial results for your customer or organization, it is well and good. It is really your obsession with work rather than result that will earn you high dividends. Result depends on so many factors other than work. Many of these factors are not in your control. So, do not let your enthusiasm for work wane because of your obsession with result. Goals and objectives are important but far more important are the daily goals and objectives in terms of work output. In undertaking any project or activity, set daily goals of work output and try to achieve them. These goals or rather targets, in any case, have to be set in keeping with the long term objective. Modern management could perhaps enrich itself if it could incorporate the philosophy of detached *karma* in its ethos.

Success and Karma

Today, happiness is synonymous with success. But success depends, inter-alia, upon the right *karma*. If *karma* is not performed to the proper extent and in the proper manner, success is doubtful. Therefore, concentrate on *karma*; do your *karma* for the sake of it– for the sake of making an offering to your deity, for the sake

of extending maximum benefit to others. Try to attain proficiency and then perfection in your work. That is what human life is all about.

Arun was a senior executive working in a PSU (Public Sector Undertaking) in India in the nineties. He was, however, not satisfied with his job because of the measly salary that he got. Many of the PSUs in India in that period were characterized by overstaffing and woefully low salaries even for their professionally qualified managerial staff. This left the employees underemployed, in technical terms. Arun was in fact very ambitious and was keen to establish some business of his own. He quit his job with the informal understanding with his management about future reinstatement, if required. He wanted to try his hand at Import Agency business. The initial spadework required to be done for establishing this business is tremendous. Arun, however, did all the spadework. He established contacts with overseas suppliers of selected products to do their marketing in India on commission terms and case to case basis. 'Case to case basis' means that he was to generate enquiries for import and endeavour to convert each specific enquiry into order. Arun worked hard to generate enquiries and negotiate order for nearly three months but, unfortunately, was unable to finalize even a single order. Over this period, though, he must have spent considerable time, money and energy. With his patience spent, Arun became exasperated and felt that it was useless to try more and perhaps he was making efforts in a wrong direction. Thus after doing so much spadework, Arun let go all his efforts to the dust. Was it the right thing to do? No, certainly not, because Arun should have tried harder.

His efforts were not misdirected, for, he had discussed the approach with established and successful businessmen before he started the venture. But Arun was so much bothered by result that he gave up too soon. This is a classic example of failure in business owing to a sheer lack of patience and perseverance. And what is this lack of patience and perseverance ascribed to? To an approach, which is not in conformity with the doctrine of *karma*, to a lack of understanding of the divine law of retribution, to the lack of faith in the justice of the Almighty God. I sincerely feel that fifty percent of business ventures fail because of this reason.

The mind rules the world but if this mind is vitiated by confusion, by needless anxiety, by attachment with reward and result and by a lack of faith in divine justice, no worthwhile efforts are going to be made. And with lack of proper efforts, success is not going to be achieved. Coming back to the case of Mr. Arun, the ambitious gentleman tried his hand at two more lines of trade but gave up midway down the effort lane. He was so much obsessed with result that with success not forthcoming, he became dejected and discontinued his efforts in sheer frustration. It is doubtful that Mr.Arun can make a success of any other business venture, given his approach. In due course of time he was back at his old job but continued to be unhappy and restless.

Focussed Karma is the Right Path

Remember, the law of *karma* operates at both levels – temporal and spiritual. Thus, for material accomplishments and material success at the lower, gross levels of living as much as for spiritual progress in the larger realm of the Almighty, the law of *karma* shows the right approach. It is, indeed, the pathway to material and spiritual progress.

When we undertake a project and meet with initial failures and setbacks, most of us tend to be discouraged and dejected. On the other hand, if we attain easy success, we exult in it. Both these states of mind viz. dejection and exultation are not conducive to material success and spiritual progress. Both disturb the peace of mind. There is subtle difference between the three emotional states of excitement, exultation and happiness. Happy person is he who does not exult in success nor grieves in failure. And when a person, through knowledge and practice, attains the balanced mental disposition in which he is unruffled by success as well as failure, he comes to possess the golden key to success. He attains freedom from attachment and gets true happiness.

I wish to reiterate that the above golden gospel of success and happiness was not invented by any man. It is the gift of the Creator to mankind. It is upon man to understand and adopt the approach shown by this golden gospel and make his life truly productive, prosperous and meaningful.

Time Management

Modern management, in its theories of optimizing the utilization of men, machines, money and time, lays down rules and methodologies of working of organizations and individuals connected therewith. In his own life, a person often finds it difficult to apply these rules. For an individual, the most important rule is that of time management. But the application of actual time management rules is not found to be easy. There are lots of problems at the mental level. The mind is the seat of all emotions and there are many types of emotions which undermine the fixity, clarity, steadfastness and stability of mind. There are many types of distractions to which a person succumbs. Because of all these factors, the person is unable to utilize his time efficiently and effectively and naturally, his productivity suffers. The key to proper time management lies in control of the excitable and irritable mind.

What Matters is Action

It should be very clearly understood that there is no substitute for hard work. Time once lost is lost forever. Learn to respect and value time. Time is a commodity which is available to each one of us alike – the poor and the rich, the brilliant and the mediocre, the young and the old. Time management has a lot to do with success and happiness because we all have limited time at our disposal in our lives. If we utilize our time judiciously, we will live well. Worry not if success does not come to you as and when expected; have the satisfaction of having made use of your time in the best possible manner. Enjoy the satisfaction of having tried and worked to the best of your ability and capacity. That is what really matters. It may be emphasized that the key to happiness lies to a great extent in the best utilization of time. The satisfaction resulting from a hard day's work is a unique feeling which no amount of wealth can provide. Try to experience it. You will begin to enjoy life as never before.

While performing a task or undertaking any project, we often tend to became impatient, restless, anxious and panicky when events do not turn out as expected. Why do such feelings come? Simply because we are much more concerned about success than about the task or its performance per se. The doctrine of *karma* as a spiritual law fully unfolds the secret of success and of failure.

Pristine Philosophy of Yoga

The law of *karma* shows the path to material success and then to spiritual salvation. It is meant for the common man engrossed in discharge of the duties and obligations of worldly life. It is for the student working hard at his high school or college level examination; it is for the restless swanky business executive; it is relevant for the painstaking teacher and it is equally relevant for the hard toiling peasant. Tools and techniques of modern management are of no value unless they are used. And they can be used only by the individual with disciplined mind. It follows that mental discipline is most important, rather crucial to proper performance of tasks and therefore, to success. Nothing is difficult, no work is impossible for the disciplined mind. Therefore, try to control that excitable mind. It is not impossible, if difficult. Proper reasoning and knowledge lays the foundation for the control of the errant mind. And then, there are a number of practical ways and means available for strengthening the hold of intellect over the mind. All these are expounded in the pristine philosophy of Yoga.

The Divine Philosophy of Karma

In the 2nd chapter, a brief description was provided of the various factors which determine success in any endeavour. To recapitulate, the various factors determining success were represented by vectorial arrows. For those readers who have studied Physics, this would be very easy to appreciate. We can also represent successful project execution through an equation of 'functions'. Therefore the success factor S can be represented in the following way.

S = f (A, B, C, D) for an activity, say a business venture project. This means the success is a function of factor A (self-efforts), B (family support), C (favourable state policy and external business environment) and, last but not the least, that great hidden, mysterious factor of luck D (no unforeseen obstructions or impediments). Here I wish to stress upon the fact that although only factor A (self-efforts) is in our control, we often falter in our efforts. The doctrine of *karma* says that we can act in an unattached mode – in a state of mind, that is focussed on the task in hand not on the reward or result. A mind focussed on the result and always obsessed by reward will be agitated or excited and never at peace. In such a state of mind, it is difficult to concentrate. But the beauty of the divine philosophy of *karma* is, that the more you concentrate on your work and try to perform it optimally, the more peaceful your mind becomes. A positive chain reaction is set in, which brings you nearer to your goals. But in practice, this tempo is difficult to maintain because of the distractions of various kinds. It is also hampered by the usual human frailties of desire, anger and attachment which are, undoubtedly, difficult to overcome.

Coming back to the main context of this book, every person seeks happiness and satisfaction through material accomplishments in the world. The words elation, jubilation and exultation do not truly describe happiness. These are impulsive, emotional states. A person exulting in success may not be truly happy. If it is ego satisfaction that he seeks in material success, he will get it. But he will be far from being satisfied and contended in the real sense. A really happy state of mind is one characterized by peace and equanimity. Thus, if a person wishes to be truly happy and derive real peace of mind, he must practise the doctrine of *karma* by trying to perfect himself in his action and duty without attachment with reward. He can set the goals but these goals should not be in the nature of material reward to his own self. They ought to be in the nature of material reward to others, who are living subjects of God.

ଓଃ୪ଚ

6. Success – More of it?

If you are not too old to recall your childhood lessons, you could, perhaps, recount your grandfather's advice – 'Hard work is the key to success'. It is an eternal truth. There is absolutely no reason on earth that you will be denied the fruits of your labour. You may not be able to choose the form, manner and time of bestowal of these fruits. But our wise ancestors had a better comprehension of the philosophy of work and success. The reward must accrue to you for all that you do. Good deeds earn good reward and ignoble deeds never go unpunished. So work hard with sincerity and devotion. In the performance of your duty, never trample upon the interests of others and maintain utmost honesty. During childhood your grandfather must have told you even this – 'Honesty is the best policy'. Honesty pays like nothing else.

In Today's Scenario

Today, things have changed quite a lot. Even if you are a highly educated professional, your peers would tend to scoff at you if you repeated your grandfather's adage on honesty. Situations, methods of work and dealings have become much more complex. It is unmistakably the 'situational management' which holds the key to success. But what is this 'situational management'? It is another name or a polished glamourised synonym of Machiavellian approach. The present world is highly competitive. Apart from the cut throat competition in the world of business, there is marked competition at the level of the individual in various spheres of life. Success has become the watchword everywhere. Go to any modern bookshop and you will find attractive titles adorning the shelves on subjects such as 'Positive Thinking', 'Successful Selling', etc. All these books are targeted at the psyche of the success hungry man of today. You will find many of these books loaded with novel formulae for success. I must say some of these books present very attractive models for success in specialized fields of endeavour and for successful living, in general. But, more often than not, there is a slip between the cup and the lip. The common man understands the approach for success. But he is often unable to overcome some inherent forces that tend to prevent him from following that approach rigorously. In this chapter, I would first endeavour to dwell upon these.

Success and Luck

Success or failure certainly depends upon the quality and magnitude of efforts in any endeavour. It also depends on many external factors and on that invisible factor called luck, as discussed in the previous chapters. But how many of us are able to actually put in optimum efforts? True, some of us are very hard working. Also, some of us are very cautious and judicious in our working. But in many cases, we are found wanting in actually performing our tasks in a manner which has been standardized as optimum in text books or guide books. The intelligent reader would at once say that it is the distractions and the frailties of our mind that undermine our efforts, as explained earlier in this book. For overcoming these problems, we have got to discipline our mind and body both. We have to first achieve good physical and mental health. Success calls for hard work, often long hours of working, day after day. There are many people who work more than twelve hours every day. Physical soundness and endurance are necessary for such hard working routine. Physical fitness can, to a considerable extent, be attained through moderation in eating, drinking, sleeping and in other activities. In fact, the key to good health is living in accordance with the divine laws of Aayurved, the ancient Indian philosophy of healthy living, a philosophy which over the years, has led to the development of various systems of medicine all over the world. All these systems of medicine are basically the offshoots of Aayurved. Regulated lifestyle holds the key to good physical and mental health. Much more important than the health of the body is the health of the mind. For keeping the mind under control and avoiding the distractions that wean us away from our regimen, Yoga shows the way. The conquest of the errant mind requires proper understanding or enlightenment, followed by proper practice. Yoga shows us the techniques which enable us to control our mind and discipline ourselves. And no task is too difficult for the disciplined self.

Honesty and Success

In this chapter, I do not wish to say anything further on the recipe for success, for, much of it is already covered by the doctrine of *karma* explained earlier. Here I would like to come back on the aspect of honesty in the performance of any task and highlight its relationship with success. What do you live for? What have you been born for? You should be very clear about the answers to these most fundamental questions. Honestly speaking, very few persons are truly aware of the answers. The answers are extremely important in the context of modern work culture and the aspect of success. For a simple explanation of the answers, it is necessary to lay down some basic facts concerning human life on this earth. Remember, man is a primordial entity and not a product of the Darwinian evolution. The origin of human life is traced to onset of *Mahayugas* (mega-ages). These *Mahayugas* are cyclic phases of time. One complete cycle of *Mahayugas* comprising *Satyug, Treta, Dwapar* and *Kaliyug,* completes itself in 4,320,000 years i.e. 4.32 million years. Since the point of origin of human life, many *Mahayugas* have elapsed. Human life has been in existence on this earth for more than 1.96 billion years according to oriental Hindu scriptures. While creating man, the Almighty God delivered to him all the knowledge that man would need to make his life worthwhile, meaningful and successful on this earth. This knowledge is contained in Vedas which are the prime source, the fountainhead of all types of knowledge of civilized life of human beings on the earth. The human life is a link in a long chain of evolution of the soul. Each link in that chain is a step in that evolution. The corporeal body is only the medium of this transit. Therefore, you have been born for providing your soul a vehicle, a medium for accomplishing its divine objective. If you lived properly, performing your tasks honestly, you would have provided a progressive ascent to your soul in pursuit of its destination. This alone is the essence of a successful life – a life devoted to righteousness. Righteousness is performance of all duty in accordance with the principles which ensure welfare of all beings in the world.

Right Approach for Material Success

Now try to extend the above broad based definition of successful living to mundane living where material success is regarded as the 'be all' and 'end all' of life. Material success is important, but many times more important is the approach you follow for attaining it. Work hard, try to earn wealth as much as you want to, but follow righteous means. Earn wealth by scrupulous means without defrauding your customer, your partner or your government. In whatever avocation you may be, try to ensure that your action does not violate the laws of the land, does not cause avoidable suffering to others and is in true accordance with the principles of *dharma* or righteousness. Making money by corrupt means may benefit you or your family in purely material terms but it is detrimental to the interest of the members of your community, your society and your nation. Success obtained by corrupt, unscrupulous means has the same character. In the long term or even in the short term, it is not going to make you happy. It must rob you of your mental peace – be sure about it. Success is a good, sweet seven letter word but you should not try to live for success. The Creator who sent you to this world also does not wish you to live for success. You only live for discharging your duties in accordance with the rules and laws prescribed by the same Creator. Understand this great truth and stop this mad pursuit of success. Instead, condition your mind on constant improvement of your methods and manners of work and duty. Success will then come sooner than expected! You will be surprised at your own foolhardiness in hankering after success even before you completed the first few steps in your ordeal.

Innovation and Hard Work

What happens when you forsake righteousness for attaining success? You either commit an illegal act or an immoral act. Both are going to land you in trouble. Acts of moral turpitude are much more in evidence today. Try to beat the competition through innovation and hard work. But here you may ask, "What is to be done if bypassing the law or violating moral principles is necessary for sheer survival?" In such circumstances, go ahead with the actions which are dictated by professional expediency to the extent they are essential to your survival. Later on, try to compensate the disadvantaged or wronged party suitably as and when opportunity arises. Immoral acts do not promote happiness. They rebound at you sooner than later to torment you.

An Example

A hypothetical life situation would highlight what has been stated above. Mr.Ramesh runs a small-scale industry in the Punjab state of India. His business involves manufacturing billet steel from iron scrap through an induction furnace. An induction furnace is a heavy power equipment that consumes enormous amount of electricity. But the unfortunate market scenario in the state is that all manufacturers of billet steel make use of 'free'

500
500
500
500
1000
1000
500
500
1000

electricity. The electricity is consumed free by suitably bribing the electricity utility officials. When all the competitors of Ramesh are employing this tactic, he cannot survive in this business by paying for electricity consumed by his furnace. So in order to remain competitive, he has to pilfer power. But Ramesh should try to donate appropriate sums of money from his profits to any public charity or otherwise to any national developmental fund. This is the way to compensate for his illegal act of power pilferage which he is compelled to do for sheer survival in the cut-throat business. Illegal acts never pay you. You must try to give back to the society or the country if you took illegally from it. Illegal and immoral acts are inimical to human happiness. They either destroy your peace of mind directly or rebound back at you in the form of miseries and adversities. You only have to practically experience such phenomena a couple of times to appreciate the truth of the law of divine retribution.

Machiavellian Approach

Strive for success and for success, employ the Machiavellian approach, also, if there be no going without it but then identify the areas where you have the freedom to act in compensation for the improprieties committed by you in the pursuit of success in this madly competitive world. If you have to bribe others to secure business do not evade government taxes – be honest there. Do not make alibis and excuses for your dishonesty. Be faithful to the society from which your material endowments came. Strive to return to the society what it gave you so bountifully. Do not be greedy and selfish. Your success is attributable in a large measure to the hard work done by others who work for you or interact with you. They and you are inseparable parts of the same society.

Success will never give you true happiness if the means employed by you for achieving it are not fair. On the contrary it will give you a feeling of guilt, self pity and even of fear, sometimes. Concentrate on what you have to do, not on what you have to get. True happiness lies in giving, not in getting. If you focus excessively on getting, you will tend to grab, wrest or snatch things because everyone else will work with such an approach. Rather than a committed, humble worker you will become an aggressive bully or a wily schemer. An atmosphere of survival of the fittest will be created in which peace, happiness and harmony are the sure casualties. You might wonder why I am disapproving the law of the survival of the fittest, a phenomenon accepted in the world since the time of Charles Darwin who propounded the theory of natural evolution. Survival of the fittest may be all right at the lower animal kingdom, but cannot fit into the human society, for, it is not conducive to harmony and peace. Where everybody strives and works for himself without properly discharging his social obligation, tensions are bound to develop in the society. The gulf between haves and have-nots will widen. It will become a society where everyone is fighting for his or her rights and very few are taking pains to discharge their duties and obligations to the society. In the process, most people are also trampling upon laws of the land. Thus in an environment marked by not only violation of law but also moral transgression, talks of peace, harmony and happiness are meaningless and hollow talks.

As per the Vedas

Ancient Hindu scriptures, the Vedas say - "Earn with thousand hands and perform charity with hundred hands". God Almighty, who created man in all his wisdom, also handed down to him the true knowledge of civilized life on this earth. The four Vedas contain all this divine knowledge which is eternal. True happiness indeed, lies in performing duty towards our brethren, in charity towards the poor, the have-nots and the downtrodden and in spending wealth for good, noble causes. It does not lie in creating more and more assets for the self. Self-aggrandizement is the worst scourge of modern civilized life. There are many who are affected by this bug. They seem to have only one obsession, only one goal – to multiply and accumulate their riches, more often than not, by means which are questionable.

Success often goes to the head of some people. It is especially the case in those situations where too much is achieved in too short a time or with relatively less effort. People begin to think that they have achieved through their great effort or by making use of their extraordinary intelligence, wisdom or courage. The moment a person begins to feel proud of his success and in the process becomes haughty and arrogant, the same moment begins his downfall. Pride blurs the intellect and once a person becomes a slave of his ego, he is bound to commit blunders and errors. Then it is only this pride which becomes the greatest impediment to his worldly success.

It is now hoped that the reader is in a position to appreciate that man does not live for success of his endeavours; he merely lives for proper accomplishment of his duties. If you performed your duties in the proper manner, you would have lived your life successfully.

7. Patience and Forbearance – Great Virtues

Wise men have always extolled patience as a great human virtue. Indeed, in the accomplishment of any task and in the performance of all worldly duties, patience is very important. Why do you lose patience? Because you are too fussy about results or obsessed with reward. There are some other reasons too why you become impatient. In the previous chapter, the necessity to follow the path of righteousness in every ordeal has been emphasized. Patience and forbearance are the foremost constituents of this righteous approach. You should not get ruffled and should maintain your mental composure in contrasting situations — like praise and censure situations or gain and loss situations. If you lose your patience and consequently your composure in such situations, you are bound to become restless and reckless. You will lose your peace of mind. But much worse, you would be liable to act imprudently and in haste and land into trouble, which means further misery. Our forefathers were indeed men of vision and wisdom. What they stated and underlined thousands of years ago is absolutely relevant even in today's world. Patience, tolerance and forbearance, indeed, are very important towards success and happiness. Impatience breeds anger and all other baneful consequences of anger. Impatience leads to foolhardy action and loss of face.

Yes, Patience is Virtue!

The virtues of patience, tolerance and forbearance have been attached so much importance in the Hindu philosophy of living, because these virtues are the pillars of progress.

A man can be patient and forbearing only if he has an unshakable faith in the law of *karma*. In fact, to perform worldly tasks in accordance with the law of *karma*, you have to cultivate patience and forbearance. Never be bogged down by unforeseen obstacles nor be discouraged by failures. Obstacles and failures are, but, stepping stones to success in the realm of the Almighty. Great inventions and discoveries in the field of science are only the result of patience. Remember Thomas Alva Edison, the great American scientist who is credited with more than 1300 scientific invention patents? His remarkable inventions were the result of painstaking efforts and a lot of patience. In today's vastly competitive world, patience has become a much more important requisite for success.

For Example

Consider the hypothetical example of Peter who is an ace tennis player. In order to win against any tough competitor, he has to exercise patience. Imagine that in a key tournament like the US Open, he is pitted against a really matching opponent. He has won two sets 6-4, 6-4 and then lost two sets at 5-7, 4-6. Now he is playing the fifth and the decider set. The stakes are high and so is the tension with a 10,000 plus crowd watching the show. Presuming that both Peter and his opponent are equally sound in the techniques of the game, the result will depend on two qualities – will to win and patience. In fact, it is a little war of nerves, a test of patience. See how important a quality patience is.

There is an old saying in India which means, 'The patient elephant gets a fat meal befitting his size but the restless and impatient dog wanders from door to door for a morsel'. It only illustrates that patience pays. It pays in all ages, in all places and in all situations. If you are patient and forbearing, you have faith in God and in His divine justice. This outlook and habit will not come instantly; it has to be cultivated by control of mind. There is lot of rigorous ordeal involved in development of this habit. But it is not too difficult. Practice makes everything possible. Sustained mental training will make it possible for you to develop a patient, forbearing approach in everything you do. Once you begin to train your mind in this manner, you will experience divine happiness, rather than mere mirth, joy or pleasure which is all temporal in nature. Experience of real happiness is synonymous to peace of mind, which has become a rare commodity. These days, billions of dollars are spent in the pursuit of this commodity but it continues to elude many people because they continue to falter in their understanding of the right and the wrong, of their duties and rights and of a moral order which is universally beneficial. What is righteousness? As stated before, it is a code of proper action, action which is conducive to universal harmony and well-being. Patience or forbearance is just one element of this code.

Another Example

When you strive hard for any goal but favourable result is not forthcoming, you tend to lose patience and peace of mind. In this context, consider the case of Mr. Anand. Mr. Anand is an Engineer, who performs the servicing and troubleshooting of advanced computer systems. One fine day, his company's MD summons him and asks him to attend to a complex fault in a client's computer system. It is a challenging task for Anand. He should be able to set right the defect as per expectations from him, as he is considered an expert in this trade. But it is also a difficult assignment because of the complexities of the computer system and the fault itself. Anand has been given a time of ten days to perform the troubleshooting work. When he sits down with the work, he spends four days wracking his brain and groping in the dark. The fault diagnosis eludes him. At the end of the fifth day, he feels exasperated and thinks he should give up. But no, there are another two days to go and he should not admit defeat so soon! With this feeling, he tries newer techniques of fault detection. Patience pays, he knows and he should not give up now after he has slogged so hard for eight days. With renewed zest and vigour, he again sets about his task.

On the tenth day, he is able to diagnose the fault and successfully set it right too. The example shows that it will be easy for you to develop an attitude towards work as an oblation to God only if you tried to be patient with regard to the result of your efforts in that work. Patience and forbearance help in control of anger too. Try to cultivate these qualities and you will find all your problems getting resolved, all your tensions getting assuaged and all your worries overcome. In all types of business and profession, these twin virtues are essential ingredients of success. And for today's average person, where there is success, there is happiness. However, let it be made clear at this juncture that true happiness results only from unattached duty — from the performance of *karma* without expectation of reward. For the true *karmayogi,* the performer of unattached *karma,* success is unimportant. So he is bound to be patient and forbearing in his tasks. But no one can become a true *karmayogi* without going through the initial rigours of mental discipline. These are the initial stages in the making of a true *karmayogi*. Ninety-nine percent of us are in those stages, where we need to develop the habit of patience and forbearance in the accomplishment of our tasks. Only then can we successfully cross these stages.

Research and Development

In today's business world, R&D (research and development) activity occupies the pride of place. In fact R&D holds the key to success in the fiercely competitive manufacturing sector. And now R&D is being extended to the non-manufacturing sectors – the services, trading, retail distribution, etc. Newer and newer softwares are being developed for achieving greater efficiency in business operations. Most of the leading multinational corporations (MNCs) are spending no less than twenty percent of their net profits on R&D. Trully, the key to survival in the future business world would be R&D. But R&D is one activity that absorbs lot of time, money and effort. The watchword in successful and effective R&D is patience. Results are not achieved easily. A great

amount of trial and error goes into a typical R&D programme. Even after spending considerable time and effort, results which could be termed tangible, often elude the R&D personnel. They have to carry on patiently. This is how research is done. This is how big MNCs have developed novel patents which are being commercially exploited in a big way. Patience is the basic factor in successful R&D.

Consider this too

Consider yet another example of the virtue of patience. A person is suffering from a severe, chronic illness. He has undertaken many different types of treatment under various systems of medicine. But he has not been benefitted. He has been running from pillar to post for months together but to no avail. He tries the treatment of one doctor, but, finding little relief, discontinues it after a few weeks. He is too impatient to stick to one particular doctor. Such a person who is having so little patience and tolerance is unlikely to be cured. Let me tell you, there are many such types of persons in today's world. They cannot stand pain and suffering from disease for long. They want some quick acting treatment, some magic potion to relieve them from their troublesome condition. They lack the patience to undertake a particular line of treatment for a reasonable period. Allopathy, Homoeopathy, Acupressure, Reiki, Yoga — there are so many systems of medicine and there are so many different types of drugs for alleviation of the suffering of the diseased. But it is quite simply the lack of patience which hinders the success of any line of treatment. A patient has to have patience. Without patience, he will find it difficult to rid himself from his ailment, to reach that cure.

Therefore, try to consciously develop these virtues which have been instrumental in great historical inventions and discoveries and technological progress. At the level of the ordinary individual, patience and forbearance have an important role in enhancing his creative faculties and in his overall physical, mental and spiritual development, besides, of course, in successful resolution of his vexing problems.

You simply recall some of the old English proverbs- 'Slow and steady wins the race' or 'Hurry makes a bad curry' and you will at once appreciate the value of patience. And then, do not forget the famous story of the man who owned the goose that laid a golden egg everyday. Driven by greed and impatience, he cut open the belly of the goose to extricate all eggs in one go.

Vision and Perseverance

Patience is crucial to proper decision making and many other functional areas of business including, of course, R&D. Business schools will not teach you the value of patience and how to cultivate it. That is one reason why qualified management graduates are performing paid jobs in business organizations and the latter are owned by men who are sometimes half-graduates or even school dropouts. Who doesn't know Bill Gates, the American business magnate who is the world's richest person owning multibillion dollar computer software industry! And there would be few, who do not know that Bill Gates is a college dropout. The great business wizards have sterling qualities like vision, foresight, a great deal of patience, perseverance and risk taking capability. These qualities are essential to business success. Here it may also be stated, that some individuals are born with such qualities but let me tell you that there are indeed many who have cultivated these qualities and performed extraordinary feats in various endeavours. It is possible to develop these sterling human qualities through mental discipline. This great truth must be clearly understood by every ordinary person who wants to rise above mediocrity and achieve great feats. Mental discipline is not an easy affair. The process of disciplining your mind starts with true knowledge or enlightenment which is to be followed by performing tasks in accordance with *dharma* or the righteous course of action. There are certain techniques and ways which help you in this. Yoga, the ancient Indian technique for disciplining mind and body is one thing which can help you enormously. Through Yogic techniques like *Praanaayaam* (breath control), you can control the errant and excitable mind. You can sharpen your sense of discrimination and make things easier for you in every endeavour.

Divine Satisfaction

I have dwelt upon the relevance of human qualities of patience and forbearance in the successful accomplishment of mundane tasks. But what has happiness to do with it? For ambitious persons, success is important but far more important than success is the manner in which it is sought, in the ways of working. Success brings happiness and satisfaction – there is no doubting it, but mere proper performance of your duty brings you not only happiness but also serenity of mind and a feeling of divine satisfaction, something which can be better experienced than explained in words.

Patience, forbearance and tolerance are extremely important for harmonious human relationships. Cultivate these qualities and I can assure you they will help you immensely to have smooth relationships with your husband or wife, with your boss, with neighbours and all others with whom you interact daily. Tolerance does not mean that you have to take things lying down; it only means that you have to avoid losing temper. There are many ways in which you can counteract brash behaviour without getting angry and, at the same time, without sacrificing your honour and prestige. With patience and tolerance, you will develop an entirely different perspective on things, a positive and progressive perspective.

ଔଷ

8. Forgiveness

You might begin to wonder whether I am attempting to dish out religious sermons on fundamental purist lines. Far from it, my sole idea is to provide a simple comprehensible framework within which it would be possible for you to develop a mental outlook and perform your daily tasks for maintaining happiness. There are many facets of such a philosophy and lifestyle. Some of them have already been touched upon, albeit briefly, in the previous chapters. But there are many more facets which need discussion, simply because these are related to our practical daily life. It is realized that sermons can never change people or can change very few people. Blank, theoretical sermonizing can have, at best, a palliative effect on the depressed and despondent individual. What is important is that he should be able to adopt the messages contained in these sermons in his life and benefit therefrom. The actual plan of action that needs to be followed in this regard is what matters most. Every person, irrespective of his educational level, intelligence quotient (IQ), financial status, race, nationality, sex, caste, creed or cultural background should be able to grasp the messages given in these sermons and much more than that, to bring about the suggested action plan into practice in his own life for the common objective of self-development and attaining happiness and mental peace.

In this chapter, another very important facet of daily behavioural life shall be discussed. This is forgiveness. Forgiveness is another great human quality. But what is its import in the context of human happiness? The following paragraphs shall throw light on the answer.

Every sane and reasonably educated person understands that harmonious human relationships are extremely important to success of any human endeavour in as much as they are the cornerstone of this success. There is little doubt that human happiness and peaceful existence depend, to a large extent, on cordial and harmonious human relationships. Forgiveness is a crucial behavioural factor in these human relationships.

The Definition of Forgiveness

What is forgiveness? If forgiveness as a virtue is extolled, does it suggest that you forgive your tormentor or pardon those who have inflicted pain and misery on you? These things need to be very clearly understood. Imagine, how many wars have been fought because of individuals' vanity and ego and how much destruction has been brought in the name of retaliation. If someone slaps you on the face, you slap him twice. In most cases, the matter does not end here. The brawl goes on with increasing intensity and the casualties are both the fighting parties. You do not often realize that squabbling is a lose-lose game. Often it is characterized by a chain reaction. The heat goes on increasing, building up yet greater tension and leading to more damage. But man, controlled and driven by that innate evil of pride, succumbs to anger and unwittingly creates situations in which he and everyone with whom he fights is the loser. Physical injury, sometimes serious, mental agony and material losses of varying magnitude are the fallout of such fights. These conflicts could be avoided most certainly, only if persons became forgiving. What kind of philosophy is behind the practical virtue of forgiveness? It is the absence of pride and consequently that of anger. Pride and anger are two of those five prime evils of Desire, Anger, Greed, Attachment and Pride which engender all sin, all misery in life. These five cardinal evils are the source of all those phenomena which are baneful for human existence. Therefore, understand and appreciate the importance of forgiveness as a human quality. Our saints have exhorted men to forgive their tormentors. There is great, divine truth in such exhortation. All spiritually great and enlightened men of history - from the time of Lord Krishna, through Buddha, Jesus Christ, Prophet Muhammad to the present generation of seers and philosophers have extolled the virtue of forgiveness. Life on this planet could be much more peaceful if all human beings endeavoured to be forgiving.

Gandhian Way

Mahatma Gandhi, the famous philosopher-saint and social reformer of twentieth century in India once said that if someone slapped you on one cheek, turn up to him the other cheek. Forgiveness is, indeed, at the core of this philosophy. If you retaliate, things can escalate or worsen. There is however, another theoretical possibility here – that of the other person hitting you again and again even if you don't hit him back. But mind you, in practice the actual probability of this is very little! So, in the final analysis, the virtue of forgiveness comes out triumphant. Here, you might argue what then is the purpose of state laws or the Police force. True, you have a right to take the help of Police or resort to legal action in such circumstances. But this does not help the cause of social harmony. It often leads to fear, suspicion and tension over long periods of time. I am aware it is extremely difficult for the ordinary person to develop forgiveness to such degree but an honest attempt in this direction is bound to prove greatly beneficial for everyone.

Forgiveness is the trait of the strong and the brave, not of the weak and the coward. Forgiveness should not be mistaken as an expression of cowardly escapism from the harsh and testing realities of situations. It is the characteristic of the brave and benevolent. Imagine how much hatred, ill-will, enmity and grudge would vanish from the world if only people became more forgiving. Retaliation and revenge are born out of anger and pride.

It is forgiveness which subdues both anger and pride and prevents the episodes of counter offence which results from the feeling of retaliation. Forgiveness is the antidote of all these evils. Violence, tension, crime, fear-psychosis and all attendant problems would reduce to a great extent if forgiveness is embraced by human mortals.

Only the Strong can Forgive

You can forgive your tormentor only if you are in a position to punish him. For being able to punish him, you have got to be strong and capable. Thus in a way, the message of being forgiving asks you to be brave and strong. It enjoins upon you to be trustful. Even persons in subordinate or inferior positions of working have their positive contribution to the society. The present division of labour in bureaucratic organizations makes every working individual's contribution essential to smooth organizational working. So every individual is important and also sometimes indispensable for proper running of organizations which today constitute the functional units of the society. Every person has a functional value and also a 'nuisance value', if put negatively. Thus everyone has the capacity to harm his tormentor, directly or indirectly. At the gross individual level, if a person is educated and well read and has good connections with people who matter, he is said to have greater bargaining power or say in various matters. Thus, he is in a better position to harm and also forgive his tormentor. All said and done, each individual in today's society has specific, important functional role in the society and, therefore, is in a position to forgive his tormentor in the interest of peace and harmony.

The concept of forgiveness may appear to be too theoretical but actually it is a very practical concept and it is meant to be brought into practice in our daily life. It is a concept which will come handy in establishing conjugal harmony and in professional advancement in this complex world of today. In the present

times, success depends to a great extent on the kind of personal relationships you maintain with others. Therefore, try to develop the quality of forgiveness. You will be much more successful and happier person. The world around you will change. Thorns will be transformed into blossoming flowers; tension will give way to peace and misery will be replaced by cheerfulness.

Wrongdoers Must be Punished

If somebody has done serious injustice to you in economic terms, you surely need to be compensated. You have every right to approach the court, file a suit and claim damages. After all, that is what legal institutions are meant for. Surely, in such cases, there is no cause for forgiveness. Imagine, that you are a trader in readymade garments. You pick up your stock lots from garment manufacturers and sell them to retailers. The garments are required to conform to standard quality specifications which have been spelt out by you when you commenced transaction with the manufacturers. The first few lots had been inspected by your quality control supervisor and found to be as per the specifications. You made the payment for twenty lots within a stipulated period of seven days. Your QC supervisor inspected only the first and the last five lots and cleared the entire consignment. Unfortunately for you, the middle lots were defective but your QC supervisor did not care to open out the cartons and properly inspect them. You discover the defective lots after the payment has been transferred to your supplier. You land up with a loss of ₹ 20 lakh because the manufacturer declined to replace the defective lots. You have only one alternative now. Approach the court and file a suit against the supplier for recovery of your money. Your retailers won't pick up these defective stocks, because they would not sell, even at reduced rates, and you are left high and dry. In such a situation, you have no business to pardon your wrongdoer. There is no question of forgiveness in these circumstances. The wrongdoer must be prosecuted.

Check It Out

Consider another example. Your house is struck by burglars and valuables worth millions are stolen. What do you do? Rightly, you lodge an FIR (First Information Report) with the police for apprehension of the culprits and possible recovery of your articles. There is no question of forgiveness here too. You should let the law take its own course. But in most situations of interpersonal behaviour, the relevance of forgiveness as a philosophy and as a personal code of conduct remains. Forgive the wrongdoer, for, he is ignorant. Forgive him, because he knows not the outcome of his acts. Some of such messages appear to come straight from our old scriptures. But they are true, universally.

In Today's Social Milieu

In the above paragraphs, it appears that I have tried to discount the need and value of forgiveness as a code of conduct in certain typical situations and that this is a deviation from the philosophy enshrined in the ancient Hindu scriptures which exhort a man to be forgiving in general. But it is not so. It is only emphasized here, that if you have been wronged, you must seek compensation. Therefore, it is important to understand the mode of application of this philosophy in today's social milieu. This is not to say that there is anything wrong with the message of forgiveness as a universal code of conduct. It is a divine message handed down to ancient humans by the Lord Creator. The supreme Creator, in all His divine wisdom, sent all true knowledge concerning human life on this earth. God is the creator of man and, therefore, quite logically, it is He who knows how human beings should interact with one another for peace and harmony, how human institutions should function, and so on. This knowledge has been handed down to His subjects by God in the Vedas. The Manusmriti provides a code of human conduct based on Vedic precepts. We know that the present age is *Kaliyug*, the age of science, technology and machines. Therefore, the divine code of conduct for the present generation has to be understood and applied in the contemporary social setting.

Swami Dayanand

Ancient Indian history is replete with accounts of spiritually enlightened and morally upright sages who forgave even their worst tormentors. You even find some such accounts in modern Indian history. Swami Dayanand was a saint and social reformer of 19th century India who is credited with dispelling much of superstition and obscurantism from the society in one of its most turbulent times. The movements started by him naturally antagonized many traditionalists and religious bigots. Many persons became his bitter enemies because his movement, though humanitarian, undermined their narrow selfish interests. One of these enemies plotted to kill the Swami. The Swami was served poison mixed in his food by his personal attendant. Swami Dayanand, on realizing that it was none other than his personal attendant who had served him poison, did not get him prosecuted or punished. Instead, he offered him a bagful of money and advised him to run away to Nepal for his life. This is a classic example of the conduct of forgiveness. Great men set examples for others to follow.

Human relationships, I would reiterate, constitute the cornerstone of the success of human endeavour. In the modern world dominated by technology, its products and by-products, cordial human relationships are at a greater premium. At the individual level, congenial behaviour is the basis of healthy and harmonious relationships. Forgiveness is indeed, an extremely important ingredient of this behaviour. Practice it and you will realize why it is so.

Applicability

It would be necessary to offer a clarification here. Forgiveness as a righteous code of conduct is applicable at the individual level only. You cannot extend it to the case of invasions and wars or similar episodes where communities, institutions and nations are pitted against one another. No, we have different code of conduct there. When our nation's freedom is in peril on account of external aggressor, it is our foremost duty to repulse the invader. All these duties have been delineated in detail in the same Hindu scriptures, the Vedas. Forgiveness has no place in such situations.

The divine Hindu philosophy of life lays down code of righteous conduct at the individual level, family level, community level, society level and at nation level. Sometimes one may clash with the other. Scriptures guide us on the applicable code of righteous conduct in all such situations.

Not to digress from our main subject of happiness, suffice it to conclude that forgiveness is a great virtue and the human individual must endeavour to adopt it in his life to make it happier, based on harmonious relationships.

9. The Price of Dishonesty

In our childhood, we are all taught to be honest. In the primary school stage, most of us are imparted lessons in truthfulness and honesty. But what do we do when we grow into adulthood? Many of us become corrupt. We often disregard honesty as a code of conduct in our day to day dealings. Some of us justify dishonest dealings as something necessary for sheer survival in the present vitiated atmosphere. Many of us resort to dishonesty out of greed or acquisitiveness. We want to make a faster buck by exploiting an opportunity to the hilt. We are obsessed by the desire for fat bank balances, palatial houses and other material things and, in this obsession, often go to any length in acquiring them. The ends become important in place of the means. Honesty is thrown to the winds.

Honesty and Happiness

What has honesty to do with happiness in the life of a human being? This chapter attempts to take a brief look at precisely this. Today you find many people who have become fabulously rich by questionable, wrongful means. Whether they acquire money through illegal trades like drug trafficking or smuggling or by tax evasion or by clever violation of other laws of the land, such money can never make them happy. It is a tried and tested doctrine. First of all, you commit illegal, dishonest acts by ignoring the qualms of conscience. Such acts are bound to vitiate your mind. Your mental peace will be disturbed and eroded. Secondly, such acts will, for sure, rebound at you in the form of adversities later on, in accordance with the doctrine of *karma*. Whatever you have acquired dishonestly, you will have to pay back to the wronged party in some form or the other and at such a time as decided

420

by God Almighty. Understand this great spiritual truth and you would realize how very stupid it is to indulge in dishonest pursuit of wealth.

For Peace and Happiness

Remember, peace and happiness is a symptom of harmony and depression and tension that of disharmony. Only righteous conduct in conformity with the definition of *dharma* as expounded by the Creator is conducive to such harmony within a man and outside him, in this world. Therefore try, consciously, not to disturb this harmony. Among the constituents of this *dharma* or righteous conduct, honesty is significant. Honesty of action promotes peace and happiness and dishonesty erodes it. There are many illustrative examples from the practical world that could be cited in support of this.

The subject of honesty has been dealt with in a previous chapter also. But there, the issue was discussed in the context of success and its relationship with human happiness. In this chapter, the matter of honest working shall be taken up in detail by dwelling upon the consequences of dishonest dealing and their baneful effect on the society and ultimately on the individual members of the society.

Many of us try to justify our dishonest actions as the 'ways of the world'. Otherwise, we are indifferent to the moral aspects of our actions. We just go on in our relentless pursuit of material things and, more often than not, do not bother whether we are being dishonest to our government or other social institutions in the process.

For Instance

Consider the hypothetical case of Amar Singh, a businessman based in the Haryana state of India. Mr. Singh owns and operates a huge factory near Chandigarh, the capital of Haryana, manufacturing bicycles. He has got a handsome turnover, exceeding ₹ 100 crores and an impressive export market for his product. In India, the excise duty on this product has been quite substantial in the range of 15 to 20 percent over the last two decades. Instead of paying the applicable excise duty honestly to the government, Mr. Singh has been resorting to the nefarious practice of under invoicing and evading huge excise duty. This is done in connivance with the local Excise Department officials, who are offered regular sums of money as bribe. This practice has been going on for years.

Divine Decree

What has Mr. Singh done? He has defrauded the government by not paying its rightful revenue running into crores of Rupees. This revenue would have been utilized by the government for running its welfare schemes for the poor or for other schemes of development. The development projects suffer a jolt and the sections of the public who were to benefit from these developmental projects are denied that benefit. Thus Mr. Singh has wronged millions of innocent citizens by evading the government's excise duty. Such actions are never conducive to happiness and peace of mind. As already stated, such illegal and also immoral actions are bound to attract an adverse reaction on the performer sooner or later as per divine decree. Mr. Singh will suffer when that adversity befalls him. He may be caught, incarcerated or punished in any other manner. Or he may suffer from some serious physical ailment. Some of his family members may have a severe illness or a serious accident. Anything may happen. Sometimes, nothing happens and one has to undergo suffering and torture in the life after death. Suffice it to say, that dishonest actions earn for you a debit entry in the ledger of your actions maintained by the Lord. Suffer you must for your sins – all the religious schools of the world are unambiguously unanimous on this. Therefore, consciously avoid indulging in dishonest acts for your own happiness and welfare, much more than the happiness and welfare of others.

Contemporary India

In India, the contemporary scene is very depressing, bordering on the disgusting. This is what one observes through the media. Lawfulness and morality in business are at a very low ebb. Some people conveniently evade laws and offer all sorts of justifications for their actions. Customs duty, Sales Tax, Income Tax, Excise duty – all are evaded on a mammoth scale. Business persons like Mr. Amar Singh who evade huge amounts of government duties and taxes are often seen grumbling into weird justification. "The government machinery is more corrupt," they often say, "Revenue raised by the government is substantially eaten up by the corrupt officials of the Public welfare or developmental schemes of the government. Then why should we pay for filling the private coffers of these corrupt officials or their political masters?"

Such perverted reasoning would be offered by many businessmen. All this has led India to this unenviable position – one of the highly corrupt countries in the world, still languishing in poverty and large scale illiteracy and occupying a deplorably low position among various countries in human development indices.

Myopic People

Short sighted or myopic persons act like Mr. Amar Singh. They do not think beyond their individual self, beyond their family and their kith and kin. To them, the society and the nation mean nothing. Here some people could blame the government for being lenient on law evading citizens or turning a Nelson's eye to them. Others could perhaps blame the extant system of governance which has led to the state of affairs. But when I am talking in terms of role and responsibility of an individual and the influence of the state systems on his mental health and happiness, I must doubly emphasize the great importance of respecting and assiduously following the laws of the land which are meant to protect the welfare of the larger population.

Remember, there is no escaping the laws of *karma*. You have indented trouble and misery for yourself the moment you have violated the law of the land, the moment you have done moral transgression. The price you have to pay for dishonesty is great. With this understanding, you would begin to have stronger qualms of conscience the next time when you are about to perform dishonest act.

Duty with Honesty

You should never offer an excuse or alibi for your dishonest acts as indicated in the above example. Never hold up the money payable by you as revenue to the government simply presuming that government machinery is corrupt. It is not your business to comment on the conduct of government officials or to sit in judgment over them. Your job is to perform your duty diligently and honestly. Imagine if everyone were to bother about his or her own duty and perform it with utmost honesty what a heaven this entire world would become!

Hypocrisy and Dishonesty

Dishonesty today exists in myriad forms, shades and hues. It exists in the general hypocrisy of action so very evident in today's global society; it exists in violation of solemn agreements in business; it exists in clever evasion of governmental taxes and duties and it exists so palpably in all those transactions of money by way of bribes and kickbacks in big national deals which harm the interests of millions of innocent persons. In the contemporary world, hypocrisy of certain nations is also quite evident in their loud pronouncement of the need for non-proliferation of nuclear weapons but secretly conducting nuclear tests and stockpiling their own weapons. Hypocrisy and dishonesty are fundamental evils of human character. Over the period of centuries, the manners and methods of wrongdoing have changed but core human evils remain at its base.

Entries in the Ledger of Karma

The doctrine of *karma* says that all our actions or *karmas* attract equal and opposite reactions. If you perform charitable acts, you will for sure, get back what you have given. If you have trampled upon the interests of your brethren or wronged them in economic terms or otherwise, you become liable to compensate them. By divine decree you will be called upon to effect this compensation. Remember those credit and debit entries in your ledger of *karmas*? Your actions make those entries and once made, these are unerasable. You must discharge your obligation to the society from which you took away so much.

National dailies in India over the past few years, not to talk of mails posted on the internet, have been providing a detailed exposition of the allegations of colossal amount of money lying in illegal accounts maintained by Indians in Swiss Banks. This money allegedly runs into US $1500 billion. India still has a substantial foreign loan burden amounting to roughly 20 percent of her GDP. If the Swiss bank money is repatriated to the home country, not only the entire loan on the country can be paid back alongwith any interest, there would be no need of loan in the future as well. If the allegations are true, a few persons have perpetrated such a great national crime by siphoning off the wealth of millions of people through unscrupulous means and stashing the wealth in faraway lands. These people are guilty of serious crime against the society and the nation. They may escape prosecution in this life but they shall have to toil in many future lives to repay their ill-gotten money to their society. They shall be born in such circumstances that they shall have to do exactly that. They shall have to undergo untold economic misery and suffering. If they have perpetuated the poverty of millions, they may have to live in rank poverty and deprivation. Nobody can escape the clutches of the divine law of *karma*.

White-collar Sinners

In olden times, thieves and robbers were viewed with contempt. But in modern times, such thieves and robbers exist as white collar criminals working covertly, who cleverly violate the laws of the land, manipulate things in their favour and get away with it. The corrupt bureaucrat, the dishonest trader, the plagiarist professional music composer, the journalist who distorts news or takes money for tailor-made articles – all belong to this category. The proportion of such thieves in the society today is far, far greater than the proportion of burglars and dacoits in the olden days. Crime and corruption today have become institutionalized. Persons who collaborate in dishonest acts frequently offer strong justification for status quo. But nearly all of these justifications are glib talks in self-deceit. How many of them actually realize the price that they will be called upon to pay for their crimes and sins? If they realized, indeed, many of them would be naturally restrained from their dishonest acts. 'The wages of sin are death,' says an ancient English proverb. The wages of dishonesty are poverty and deprivation. How can you be happy if you are afflicted by poverty? Be very clear on this. The edifice of happy life is built upon a foundation of moral and righteous acts. There is no escaping this great truth, this divine law.

Importance of Moral Science

Moral science is a neglected science today. Can anyone dispute this? We used to impart our young children formal lessons in ethics and morality during their primary level schooling. But the trend has significantly come down. The importance paid to moral education has decreased for some really strange reasons. The need for moral code of conduct is far greater today, though. But what exactly has morality to do with human happiness? It has a lot to do. Eminent psychologist Sigmund Freud had said that the secret of happiness lay in loving well and working well. He meant that a man needs to have good relations with his friends, peers and relatives and derive optimum satisfaction from his professional working in order to be really happy. But did he spell out exactly how a person can develop and maintain cordial relations with others and at the same time perform his daily work to his full satisfaction? The answers are provided by the age-old moral code of conduct expounded in Manusmriti and of course, our famous doctrine of *karma* enunciated in Bhagwadgita. The moral code of conduct which exhorts man to adopt such virtues as forgiveness and patience is not to be narrowly viewed as a religious or sectarian code. It is the fundamental, universal philosophy of proper and successful living. This fact has to be very clearly understood. No amount of psychoanalysis can help the troubled mind as much as a plan of righteous action in accordance with the above code, based as it is on the definition of man as a material cum spiritual entity. Remember, when you commit dishonest acts, you automatically invite an adverse reaction on your mind. The mind is a material entity. It tends to be easily disturbed. It is excitable, irritable, flexible. You can always endeavour to control it through techniques of *yoga*. But through moral discipline and adherence to the righteous code of conduct, you will make way for healthy impressions and stimuli on the mind. Such stimuli would make mind calm and serene. They will make you happy and enable you to truly enjoy your life.

Human Greed

On this beautiful earth, the Lord God has provided sufficient resources far satisfying the needs of every human being. But can human greed ever be satisfied? This greed had impelled persons to invade alien territories, indulge in unnecessary wars and plunder the wealth of the vanquished countries. The present global society shows extremes of riches and poverty in which greed as a factor cannot be discounted. There are glaring inequalities of comsumption. Even now, at the dawn of the twenty-first century, these inequalities are clearly visible. Almost twenty percent of the world's population consumes eighty percent of the global material resources.

Unless we remove the element of dishonesty from our conduct, peace and happiness would remain a far cry. One must admit that the path of righteousness is thorny and difficult to tread but there is no gain without pain. Pain and penance are the foundation of spiritual progress.

ଔ

10. Purity of Body and Mind

God Almighty created this planet earth and the earthlings– the various plants, animals and human beings. He, in His infinite wisdom, handed down to the earliest humans the knowledge of healthy, happy and meaningful living. Referring to the divine code of righteousness or *dharma*, purity of body and mind is another element of this code.

What is implied by purity of body and mind and how is it related to human peace and happiness? This chapter provides the answers.

Dangers to Human Health

Purity of body is necessary for maintaining good health. Cleanliness, it is said, is next to Godliness. The importance of external cleanliness in our surroundings and environment is, perhaps, too well known. Clean and wholesome environment, hygienic conditions of living and proper sanitation are essential to good health. Today, these factors are being attached greater importance than ever before with increasing danger to global environment from industrialization. The dangers posed to human health from industrial effluents, vehicular smoke, polluted water and food along with other artificialities of life are many and serious. They undermine physical and mental health and their deleterious effects sometimes make human life miserable. Good health is one of the very important requisites of happiness and success in life. The purity of body can be maintained by following the rules of healthy living laid down in Aayurved, the ancient oriental science of health and longevity. Here it would be relevant to mention that all the systems and practices of medicine in vogue are derived from the vast ocean of Aayurved. Be it Allopathy or Homoeopathy or Naturopathy or Accupressure therapy, all the known systems of medicine are leaves taken from the chapters of the divine science of Aayurved. What is the basis of this statement? Aayurved is as old as man himself. Aayurved is the knowledge given to man by man's Creator. Who is better knowledgeable about a machine than its Engineer who designed and constructed it? He knows best how to maintain it. He alone prepares its troubleshooting manual. Similarly man is the creation of God and God alone knows how to maintain His objects of creation in the best of health, fitness and efficiency.

The knowledge provided by Him is the ultimate knowledge on human health and longevity. We must respect it, understand it and apply it for our own benefit. Purity of body calls for following a regimen which keeps the body clean and free of disease causing bacteria, viruses and fungi. Remember, no pathogenic microbes can survive in a clean and healthy body. Maintenance of this cleanliness and purity of our bodies is what is enjoined upon us. Aayurved shows us the best approach for this. It shows us that human beings can be categorized into seven different types of constitution and it prescribes proper diet and other lifestyle regimen for each constitution type. It reveals to us that following the correct diet and other lifestyle regimen in accordance with one's constitution or *prakriti* keeps at bay the fundamental disease causing process. Aayurved enlightens us on the effect of sun, wind, rain and various seasons on our body mechanisms. Above all, it reveals to us the remarkable medicinal values of thousands of natural herbs, minerals, metals and many other substances.

Yoga is an important technique of disciplining mind and body and thus keeping them clean, pure and healthy. This ancient science contained in Hindu scriptures and systematized by sage Patanjali, enjoys immense popularity even in today's world among the various sections of the human population.

Purity of Body

Good health is essential for a successful life and a happy life. And bear it in your mind that keeping yourself in the best of health is largely in your own hands. Purity of body can be maintained by sincerely following the basic rules of healthy living stated in Aayurved. But the sad fact is that many of us are either ignorant of these rules or have little faith in the philosophy of Aayurved or are too lazy and self-indulgent. By leading a life of indolence and self-indulgence, we keep on violating these most basic rules of health and invite trouble for ourselves in the form of disease. Disease may manifest itself on the physical plane or on the mental plane. In both cases, it plays havoc with happiness and kills the joy of living.

Startling Facts

Consider a few startling facts. Today, at the dawn of the twenty-first century, man is still fighting against the scourge of many intractable diseases like Cancer and AIDS. In the developing countries, Tuberculosis and Leprosy still afflict people in large numbers. Many serious infectious diseases are making a resurgence because their pathogenic germs or bacteria are increasingly becoming drug resistant. Bacteria are forming newer and newer strains which are resistant to the antibiotics presently used. So new types of antibiotics are being developed by medical and pharmaceutical researchers. Modern medical science has been vanquishing many diseases but, at the same time, newer and unheard of diseases are cropping up, as if from nowhere.

This kind of situation only suggests that somewhere our knowledge and techniques of healthcare are deficient. We have to take guidance from the divine health-science of Aayurved which contains the solution to every health problem of man. The basic, simple rules of healthy living expounded in Aayurved are intelligible and practicable. We should pick them out, closely

follow them and maintain our lifestyle in accordance with these rules so that we may successfully prevent disease and enhance longevity. Prevention is better than cure but even if disease strikes us, the best solution can be provided by following a holistic approach to treatment – by drawing upon the best and useful from all systems of medicine which are but offshoots of Aayurved. It is imprudent to harbour prejudices against certain systems of medicine.

Approaches to treatment of disease in various systems of medicine appear to be quite different but they all seek to attain the same end result. The best way is to recognize that no therapeutic system is perfect. Each one has deficiencies, some of which are the result of our imperfect understanding of the nature of diseases, their inception and cure. The best approach is a holistic approach in which you pick on the best and the useful from each system of medicine for adopting in the lifestyle and for treating diseases as required.

Wholesome Health

It has to be understood by the intelligent individual that no pathogenic bacteria, viruses or other microorganism germs can thrive in a clean and wholesome body. It is upto us to keep our bodies wholesome and pure. And fortunately the fundamental rules for doing it are known to us. Aayurvedic texts provide a succinct account of these rules. We only have to shed our bias, if any, against them and follow them. Aayurved says that good health requires keeping the three basic humours - *kapha* (phlegm), *pitt* (bile) and *vaat* (wind) of the body in proper balance and preventing their vitiation. Purity of body and mind does not connote maintenance of mere cosmetic cleanliness. It means the body needs to be internally clean and pure with functional humours (*doshas*) and tissues (*dhatus*) in optimum working condition. This can be brought about through right diet, moderation in food, sleep, work, exercise and sex and maintaining a state of mind free from excessive ambition, hatred, jealousy and sinful thoughts. Our learned sages and savants of the yore were indeed men of vision and wisdom. What they have written down in their treatises or passed down by words of mouth to the succeeding generations is the gospel truth – the true knowledge which is sourced to God, the fountainhead of all knowledge. When they said purity of body and mind is essential to good living, they meant exactly to dissuade mankind from violating the supreme laws of health enunciated in Aayurved.

Aayurved and Health Care

It needs to be reiterated that much confusion still prevails in the contemporary world on the true cause of disease and the true path to cure. This is evidenced by the numerous different schools and systems of medicine with their medical men working in almost closed, watertight compartments. A conscious belief in the primacy of Aayurved as the true fundamental science of medicine and health care is necessary to carve out the holistic and middle-of-way approach to health care. In this approach, most important things are discipline of the body and mind. Regular habits of sleep and food intake and moderation in work, exercise and other living habits go a long way in effectively preventing disease.

Saatvik Food

In achieving purity of the body, it is of utmost necessity that our food should be *saattvik* i.e. light, natural, clean, bland and, obviously, vegetarian. The virtues of vegetarianism are now becoming clearer to millions across the world. Most importantly, it is the medical scientists and nutritional experts who are advocating vegetarianism. It has been scientifically established that man is intended by nature to be vegetarian. This is borne out by the shape of his teeth, length of his intestine and the manner of his drinking water which are similar to those of herbivorous or frugivorous animals. Man is, in fact, also a frugivorous mammal. Fruits are the best items of *saatvik* food. Milk is yet another. These are the foods, which cleanse the bloodstream and tissues of poisonous humours. Fruits are the substances that man naturally likes to eat in the raw, original, pure state. But can he eat raw meat? Man's natural abhorrence to raw meat as a food is reason enough to convincingly prove that man is a born vegetarian. Vegetables, cereals, pulses, nuts and herbs are the items of food that make the healthy, vegetarian diet of man. Mental health is, perhaps, more important than physical health. Mental ill health may result from a variety of causes, some of them grossly corporeal. When the causes are physical or corporeal, these involve vitiation of *doshas* (body humours) and their morbid flow towards the brain. Such diseases are best diagnosed and treated by those trained in Aayurvedic therapeutics. But in a large majority of ordinary cases, mental illness is the result of negative, impure thought. Purity of mind has to be achieved by dispelling morbid thoughts and thought processes.

The first pollutant of mind is envy. Simply stated, the antidote of envy is love. Honestly pose a question to yourself. Do you feel happy and elated at the success and prosperity of your friends, peers, kith, kin, neighbours? If not, you also suffer from the mental morbidity called envy. Defeat this morbid element of envy with love. Develop love with everyone – young or old. Love kindles and accentuates the joy of living.

Cruelty and Selfishness

The second pollutant of the mind is cruelty. Cruelty stems largely from selfishness. Today, we find self-oriented and self-centered people in large numbers. With such narrow approach, these people keep on worrying about their own selves constantly. They are ever engrossed in their own problems, real or imaginary. They show little time or concern for attending to others' cries for help. They remain cold, aloof to the problems of the poor, deprived and the downtrodden. They often display an inhuman cruelty towards their fellow beings when they are actually in a position to alleviate their misery. Be very clear on this– a selfish person is an unhappy person because all his attention is focused on his own self, his own problems and material issues. He may have the time and resources to help others but has no inclination for rendering such help. Go and try to help out of your way a destitute, a downtrodden and you will experience a sense of divine happiness. Such benevolent acts will also do a lot to assuage your tension and worries. If you are afflicted by depresion, visits to the psychiatrist may or may not help. But charitable acts would certainly and always help to soothen your despondent mind.

Anger and Sin

The third important pollutant of the mind is anger. A previous chapter has already provided a detailed account of this emotion, which poisons the mind and leads to many types of sinful acts. But here, an indirect approach to controlling or conquering anger is suggested. Disregard your tormentors and you will find anger will never take hold of you. Try consciously to develop an attitude of indifference and disregard towards those who may torment you by their wicked actions or offensive behaviour. You will not be overcome with anger. And once you have learned to control anger, you would have spared yourself a lot of misery.

Mundane Misery

Every human mortal who has been ushered into this world has a right to healthy and happy living. But in actuality it is seen, that there is lot of disease, pain and misery in this world. Misery of all kinds is the result of human misdeeds i.e. unrighteous actions. Therefore, every sane and right thinking individual must understand the importance of following the code of righteous conduct, for, that alone is the passport to happiness and prosperity. Remember, disease and ill health too are the result of bad *karma* or sinful conduct in the past. Nobody can escape from the clutches of his own past *karma* which determines his fate. Suffer he must for his misdeeds but he must draw upon the wisdom and knowledge of our ancient sages and seers and endeavour to perform all action rationally, righteously and virtuously. The human mind is vitiated by certain other elements too. These shall be briefly discussed before bringing this chapter to a close.

Hatred and Mind

What do you think about the element of hatred? Why and wherefrom does this element creep into the human mind? When somebody has duped you, insulted you or wronged you in any other way, you tend to develop hatred towards him. But what happens when this feeling of hatred settles or starts growing? It positively disturbs your peace of mind. It makes you tense and unhappy. This again is human nature. You tend to feel happy and cheerful if people around you respond amicably to your calls or react in a manner favourable to you. If not, you naturally tend to be disturbed. But this unhappy feeling takes hold only if you harbour a certain dislike or hatred towards your tormentor. If you overcame this feeling of hatred, you would never feel upset or unhappy. Thus the true cause of unhappiness here is hatred. Try to defeat hatred by love. Try consciously to love even your enemy.

Practical Religion

Religion is meaningless and useless if it is confined to blank theoretical sermons. True religion is practical and it shows you how to become a better human being, how to make the best out of your life of limited time span and how to realize the supreme God through physical and mental training, discipline and spiritual development. Let the message of shedding hatred not be taken as a theoretical religious sermon. It needs to be taken as a part of the practical regimen of successful human living. You should try to love everyone, including your detractors and enemies. But this does not mean you should willy-nilly fall into the trap of your wicked enemies or play into their hands. No, you should always safeguard your own interest but never hate your fellow beings for their inhuman acts. Hate the sin, not the sinner, for, the sinner sins out of ignorance.

This takes us to another mind polluting element – the old familiar evil of greed! Yes, greed of material things breeds a lot of misery. There is an end to human need but there is no end to greed. Greed is like the ever growing monster which can only die a catastrophic death – it can only burst when it gets bloated beyond the mental and physical capacity of the person whom it grips.

Greed breeds multiple evils. It engenders crime and corruption of varied types and shades. It creates social disharmony and tension. In chapter no.2 (High Ambitions), an account was given of how unrealistically high ambition can play havoc with the mental peace of human mortals. Greed perverts the mind; it drives and induces a man to sin for the acquisition of his objects of desire. Healthy ambition is good and conducive to human development but greed is devilish. It slowly but surely takes man to the door of hell. The Hindu philosophy of living condemns greed as a cardinal evil. It suggests that we reasonably restrict our desires so that we may not fall a victim to the evil of greed. In this world there is enough to satisfy everybody's need but not enough to satisfy everybody's greed. For, it is only greed that has given birth to forces of loot and plunder and of corruption which includes white collar crimes. Greed will drive you to sin which would bounce back at you with adversity sooner or later. The importance of purity of the body and the mind for healthy and happy human existence has been described in the foregoing pages and paragraphs. It brings to a close a most humble attempt to discuss a subject which has depth greater than the oceans and horizon greater than the skies.

METAPHORICAL REPRESENTATION OF A HUMAN BEING

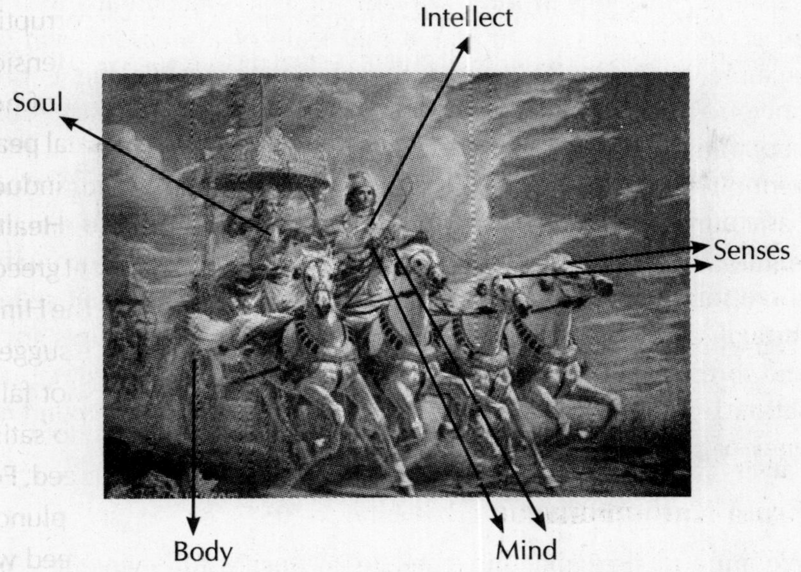

A human being is a physical body plus mind plus intellect plus soul; these elements are metaphorically represented in the above picture.

11. Control of the Senses

What is the purpose of our existence? Why were you and I ushered into this world? Was our birth a spontaneous event, an accidental episode or was it the result of a divine design of a supreme, infinitely powerful entity that controls the entire universe? For every one of us who desires true peace and happiness and wishes to make a true success of his life on this earth, it is necessary to know answers to all these questions. The basic purpose of our life must be clear to us. Otherwise, it is merely vegetable existence that we shall lead. We have been born with some inherent physical and mental weaknesses; we shall swim through the turbulent ocean of life with its successes, failures, joys and sorrows and then die one day. How many of us have the true satisfaction of having led successful lives purely from the point of view of our duties?

From Kathopanishad

We must realize that the essence of successful living lies in performing our duties properly and righteously all through our life. Therein lies also the secret of happiness. It was briefly explained in an earlier chapter that our life is just a link in a chain of births and rebirths. Each birth sets forth a journey through this material world, performed by the soul for attaining greater refinement till it finally attunes with the supreme soul or God. It is in this context, that a verse from Kathopanishad, a Hindu scripture, is relevant.

Body: A Divine Chariot

"The human being is similar to a chariot driven by horses; the body of the chariot is the human corporeal body; the horses steering the chariot are the human senses; the bridle of all these horses is the human mind; charioteer who holds this bridle is the human intellect and the traveller seated inside the chariot is the human soul." It is a perfect analogy for anyone who wishes to understand the true nature of a human being and also the true purpose of living. Life is a voyage through time for the soul which seeks freedom from bondage and misery. When this freedom is attained, it no longer requires to reside in a human body because it is qualified to enjoy bliss in tuning with God.

Explanation of the Analogy

From the above analogy it is clear that the purpose of human life would be fulfilled or the human life would have been successfully lived, if the soul is steered in the right direction towards its ultimate objective i.e. God. This is possible only if the intellect (charioteer) guides the senses (the horses) properly. The medium of control of the senses is the mind (the horse bridle) which has to be regulated and subdued. If the bridle (mind) is let loose, the horses (senses) shall go astray. Therefore, control of the senses through regulation of the mind is the important thing. The senses have a tendency to go astray because the mind itself is excitable and corruptible. We have to control this errant mind by exercising the force of our intellect. This, in brief, is the essence of a successful living and thus a happy living.

How do our senses behave and what kind of control needs to be exercised over them? We all know from our daily experience that we like to hear words in our praise, touch and see sensual objects, devour delicious delicacies which may be potentially harmful for our health and use fragrant cosmetics to enhance our physical appeal. How each of these undermines our well being and happiness would be explained in the following pages.

Flattery and Ego

As stated above, we have a natural tendency to hear words in our praise. Flattery pleases most of us. But this is exactly where we have to restrain ourselves. Flattery nurtures our ego and, therefore, is to be shunned. Anything which bloats our ego is detrimental to our interest because inflated ego creates multiple problems. It breeds a false sense of pride, vitiates the intellect and weans us away from the progressive course of action. Therefore, avoid lending ears to flattery. Another area where restraint needs to be exercised in using our hearing faculty is in listening to others' censures. This is something we should try to avoid. If we listen to words in censure of others, it will only serve to engender feelings of hatred and anger. Why invite these evils at all if they can be avoided? Remember, it is always difficult to get over hatred, envy, pride and anger because these are the frailties of the human mind. But there is an approach, whereby many of these evils can be prevented from taking hold of us. And prevention is always better than cure! Restraint, in a prudent manner, in the use of our physical senses helps to keep these evils at bay. What else is forbidden material for listening? Anything said in derision of God, pious men and scriptures which are sacred. If we hear all this, it will tend to undermine our belief and faith in God and wean us away from the virtuous path. It is also desirable that we avoid listening to talks about ostentatious lifestyles of others because that is bound to work up our greed.

In the prudent use of our physical senses lies the way to real happiness. Again, this is a very practical matter and we have to actually follow this divine sermon to experience the real joy of living.

Pre or Extra-marital Sex

The sense of touch also needs to be properly controlled. The first and the foremost area in which restraint is needed is physical contact with person of opposite sex other than spouse for the purpose of sensual pleasure. This, undoubtedly, is a very controversial matter. In many societies of the world, pre-marital and extra-marital sex is common and the society does not disapprove of pre-marital sex at least. However, extra-marital sex or adultery is condemned to a larger or smaller degree in most of the global societies. In conservative societies of Asia and especially South Asian countries, sexual contact with person of opposite sex outside of marriage is strongly proscribed and condemned. Extra-marital affair plays havoc with the institution of marriage and creates social disharmony. And social disharmony is never conducive to individual happiness and progress too. Pre-marital sex, wherever it is prevalent, has led to a host of problems. It has endangered the healthy growth and development of youngsters, especially teenagers and badly exposed them to the scourge of diseases like AIDS. Here it may be sufficient to say that in view of what is stated above, sexual discipline is an essential requisite of human health and happiness.

Sense of Touch

The need for disciplining the sense of touch does not end here. Too many physical comforts should also be avoided. For example, the use of soft bed and pillows encourages indolence, it tends to make a person inactive and undermine his productivity. It impedes his overall progress. Have you not experienced that if you sleep for ten hours during a night instead of your normal quota of seven hours, you tend to feel lethargic and drowsy during the following day? Soft beds and pillows, air-conditioners, room heaters etc. only induce a tendency towards greater rest, greater sleep. These devices should be used in moderation. The ideal thing is to use a comparatively hard bed. But to the extent practically possible, the use of such things should be minimized. Remember, the use of extra soft cushions for beds and pillows is also not medically recommended. Persons suffering from spinal problems like spondylitis are advised to sleep on hard beds and sit on cushionless chairs. Control of the sense of touch extends to many other areas of our daily life. For example, the scriptures indicate that you should not touch stolen wealth in any form. This has a very broad connotation. It suggests that you should not touch anything which has been procured by wealth generated through corrupt means or anything which helps you to generate such wealth. Imagine how

many articles become forbidden to touch thereby! True, we all know in our hearts where we have sinned. We all know how much corrupt dealing we have done and where. You surely know how much income tax or sales tax you evaded last year and where you have kept the unaccounted or 'black' money or what all you have purchased with it. If you and I start following the above dictum in letter and spirit by strictly avoiding the touch of ill gotten wealth and every physical article purchased through it, the whole world would turn into an economic paradise in a short time. But alas, that does not happen! The path of morality, of righteousness is thorny and difficult. But this path has to be followed for lasting happiness and peace

Sense of Sight

The third sense of ours is the sense of sight. Here again we need to exercise restraint. We should not look at objects of sexual lust lest it should violate our sexual continence. The importance of sexual continence or *brahmacharya* has been greatly emphasized in Hindu scriptures. Sexual continence has been stated to be the foundation of physical and mental strength and of spiritual development. Lack of sexual discipline is the root cause of many human problems. It weakens man physically, mentally and morally. So, refrain from using your sense of vision for seeing objects with sexual lust.

Sense of Taste

The sense of taste makes use of tongue. The tongue is the starting point of the route of ingestion of our food. The tongue should be used for intake of such food as is in agreement with our natural constitution or *prakriti*. As per Aayurved, any food not in accordance with individual *prakriti* causes disease. Therefore, intake of food compatible with *prakriti* or constitution is the first and the foremost golden rule for good health. This point has already been touched, albeit obliquely in the previous chapter. The second point of importance in judicious use of the tongue is the need of moderation in eating and drinking and in avoidance of *taamasic* substances like meat and liquor. *Taamasic* refers to such substances which defile the body and corrupt the mind. The deleterious effects of the intake of meat and liquor on the body have been described in Aayurved and are being acknowledged by modern medical men and nutritional experts too. The intake of meat and liquor has been implicated in the development of such death dealing ailments as heart disease, strokes and cancer. So, prudence suggests that you avoid intake of the proscribed items of food and exercise restraint over your taste buds accordingly!

Sense of Speech

Apart from eating and drinking, the tongue is also involved in speaking. What kind of speech can land you in trouble and spoil your peace of mind or can put obstacles in your progress? Avoid a speech which casts aspersions on others, for, it will generate hatred, enmity and anger. It is detrimental to both speaker and listeners. Further, do not use your tongue in self praise or boasting. It weans you away from the path of righteousness or *dharm* by bloating your ego. Also, avoid flattery of others. It undermines your own strength of character. Do not indulge in idle, needless gossip and also refrain from speaking untruth. These acts also do not promote righteous conduct and action. Then, also try to avoid making sarcastic, harsh and insulting remarks. Such remarks are extremely saddening and displeasing. If you speak to a person in such a manner he feels miserable and often curses you. There are some more areas where restraint needs to be exercised in the use of your sense of speech. Do not use demeaning and obscene words. They pollute the mind. And never slander your teachers and preceptors, scriptures, the holy men and saints and the parents. It erodes faith and mutual confidence and encourages brash behaviour.

What is stated in the above lines looks like a leaf out of a typical scripture. But the significance of messages contained in scriptures should be understood. They are all meant to help you through the turbulent ocean of life, to illuminate your arduous and darkness ridden path and to provide you true knowledge of the approach towards a successful and happy life.

Sense of Smell

The sense of smell is to be used to discard foul smelling objects which are the source of disease causing germs or to avoid objects which pollute the body. The use of too many artificial perfumes and scents should also be avoided as they delude the sense and the user is unable to discriminate between dirty pollutants and clean substances. The prudent use of the sense of smell is important for maintaining cleanliness, hygiene and good health.

Whatever actions we perform in this world are done through our senses. All good deeds, bad deeds, sinful acts, benevolent acts are performed through these senses. Judicious use of these senses can save us from all the misery, all the failures, all the tensions and problems that we know. This judicious use means use in accordance with the supreme principles of *dharma* or righteousness described in Manusmriti. These great truths must be understood by all of us who seek happiness, success and fulfillment in life. A most important point needs to be mentioned here before bringing this chapter to a close. With your sense of speech, utter the name of Almighty God daily and pray to Him that he may provide you the intellect and the strength of character so that you never deviate from the right path, the path of *dharma*. With your other senses, endevaour to perform noble, virtuous acts. This message is given by all religious schools and sects of the world. Remember God by any name, in any language. He is one and supreme. He created all of us and in His infinitely great wisdom, handed out to us a code of right living. This code has to be understood, respected and followed. This code will help you to maintain your body and mind in healthy condition and to achieve the development and refinement of your spirit in the process of its divine perfection.

ଔଡ଼

12. Intellect – Its Role and Importance

Intellect is the most important entity in a human being, next only to the soul. It is through intellect that we are able to discriminate between right and the wrong, between truth and untruth, between devil and the saint. You might make a naive inference that each one of us is gifted with an intellect capable of perfect discrimination. This is not the case. Some folks have a sharper intellect than others. They are able to comprehend truth more easily. They are able to judge things better than others. But each one of us possesses a faculty of basic intellect which can be used to control the excitable mind. A wise man is one who knows what is right and acts accordingly, whether he has the mental inclination or not for that action. But a foolish man acts according to his mental propensity. He may or may not understand the truth. Even if he is enlightened on the proper course of action, he tends to act out of sheer impulse or whims and follows his mental inclination. Intellect has a major role in all our actions. Its role is twofold – comprehension of the truth and control of the errant mind. The mind is liable to deviate from the right course of action. It is the intellect which controls the mind.

The esoteric relationship between the mind and the intellect known, you only have to bridle your mind through the sheer force and strength of your intellect to do proper action which is conducive to your worldly progress and spiritual advancement. It is in your overall progress that true peace and happiness lies.

Factors of Influence

The intellect as a faculty is subject to a variety of influences. The intellectual level of different persons is different. Modern psychologists call it difference in IQ (Intelligence Quotient). This

IQ level is the measure of intellectual prowess we are born with. There is not much we can do to improve it. But, actually, it is the application of this intelligence which is more important. How many people use their intellect judiciously? Not very many! The intellect itself is liable to be clouded very often.

Many phenomena in the physical medium and the spiritual medium profoundly affect the intellect. Influences coming from these media are the result of your good or bad actions, sinful or virtuous deeds. If you perform virtuous deeds, your intellect will receive positive influences which will help you to think creatively, constructively and properly. On the other hand, if you indulge in falsehood, deceit and other vicious acts, the influence on your intellect shall be banal.

Dharma enjoins upon us to make use of our intellect in the proper manner. The important thing is to keep control over the mind and regulate the use of the sensory organs.

Consider This

Let us take the case of Mr. Iqbal. Mr. Iqbal is a thirty-five years old busy executive in a multinational corporation. Of late, he has been having some problems with his health. He doesn't find himself as fit and energetic as he was some two to three years ago. He gets himself thoroughly examined by a doctor. The doctor finds nothing seriously wrong except mild hypertension and overweight. Mr. Iqbal is found to be 25 percent overweight and is strongly advised to change his sedentary lifestyle and perform regular exercise for at least half an hour every day. It is particularly important for him because he has a family history of heart disease for which obesity and sedentary living are strong predisposing factors.

Mr. Iqbal decided to start regular morning walk. On the first three days, he was quite regular. He got up in the morning in time and went for his brisk walk. On the fourth day, he didn't feel like getting out of the cozy comfort of his bed. The same thing happened on the fifth day too. Crouched in his bed, Mr. Iqbal is aware that his indolence or lethargy is going to do him harm but he stays on in his bed. Here is an interesting interplay of mind and intellect. The intellect of Mr. Iqbal is fully aware of the grave need to perform daily morning exercise. But his mind acquiesces to the desire to have more comfort, more rest. The mind is errant. It has to be controlled by the intellect. The strong will power needed to control the errant mind has to come from within, through spiritual strength. But in the case of Mr. Iqbal, this will power is wanting. The excitable mind lets loose the control over his body and his sensory organs. And the result is that he is unable to regulate his daily life. His health will further deteriorate. He is painfully aware of this but knowing fully well the remedy, is unable to organize himself for his daily suggested routine of physical exercise. The mind defeats a person. The mind if properly controlled, takes a person to the pinnacle of success and glory. But it can, as well, take him to the mouth of hell. The intellect knows what is proper and improper; only it has to be activated and strengthened to control the mind. There lies the secret of successful and happy living.

Look at this too

Consider another example from our daily life. Mr. Vivek is an inveterate alcoholic. Failing health in recent weeks has put a limit or his intake of alcohol. But Mr. Vivek is so much addicted that he disregards his physician's advice and does not curtail his liquor intake. The result is left to your imagination. This is another case of weakness of the will power. The intellect knows what is right but fails to hold the mind and the senses from going astray. In fact, the whole life of ours is a saga of the interplay between the mind and the intellect. Intellect is the controller of mind. This intellect, in turn, is powered by our own self – the soul. The will power referred to above is nothing but our own spiritual strength which needs to be exercised. But when we let our mind float freely, we become a slave to it. When we become a slave to our mind, we truly become something like a rudderless ship. Through the intellect we know what is right and what is wrong. Still we do not follow the right path. We find it difficult to pull our strings together and get set into a regimen of hard work, simply because we remain slaves to our passion, our desires and our emotional impulses. It is these we have to conquer. Reason should become not only our guiding force but our driving force too. Put the engine of your life with your intellect. Let all driving impulses come from the intellect, not the mind. But this in practice is far from easy. Human life is the battleground for this duel between the mind and the intellect. For those of you who have guided their lives with solid reason and steered themselves on the right course in accordance with enlightened reason, the life has been a successful ordeal.

Temptation

You know of a term called temptation. Temptation is of various types - Temptation for evading taxes, temptation to accept bribes, temptation for drugs and cigarette, temptation of liquor, temptation for extra-marital flings et al. The basic factor behind temptations of all kinds is the mind. The moment mind is let free, it becomes subject to the forces of passion working through the five senses. They all seek pleasure, gratification and enjoyment in purely material terms. The faculty of intellect sitting at the back knows that all these indiscretions are baneful and will bring harmful effects. But it lies there like a lame duck – powerless and ineffective. So, make your intellect effective and powerful. Those of you who are more analytical and curious might ask – What is it that comes between mind and the intellect? Which entity shall work towards making the intellect dynamic and powerful so that it effectively controls the mind? As already mentioned before, the answer to both these questions

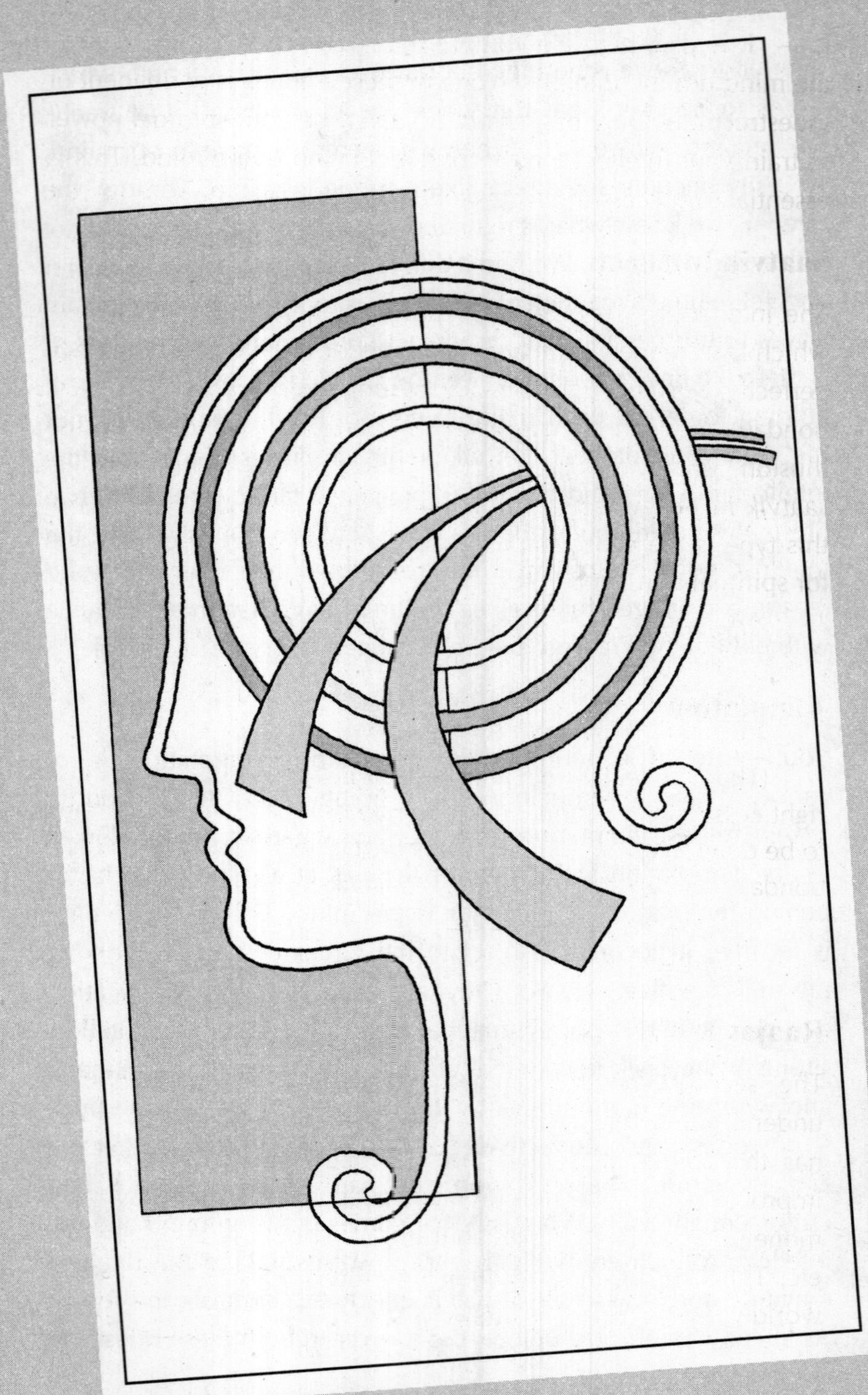

is – It is you, because you are the soul, not the body, neither the mind nor the intellect. None of these entities is permanent or indestructible. Only the soul is. So, exercise your spiritual power to train your intellect for effective regulation of the mind. This is essential to successful, healthy and happy living.

Saatvik Intellect

The intellect too is of varied types and character. That intellect which is so refined, pure and developed as is able to discriminate perfectly between righteous and wrong action, virtue and vice, bondage and liberation, truth and untruth and between reality and illusion, is of the highest order. This kind of intellect is called *saatvik* in Bhagwadgita, the famous Hindu scripture. Intellect of this type is the contrivance for achievement of higher goals and for spiritual transcendence.

Pravrittim ch nivrittim ch
Kaaryaakaarye bhayaabhaye
Bandham moksham ch yaa vetti
Buddhih saa paarth saatvikee !!

(That intellect which knows what is right action and what is right cessation of action; what must be done and what ought not to be done, what is fear and what constitutes fearlessness, what is bondage and what is liberation, is Saatvik in nature)

(Shrimad Bhagwadgita,
shlok # 30, chapter # 18)

Raajasik Intellect

The second type of intellect is one which is capable of understanding the intricacies of the material world and which has the power of discriminating between the proper and the improper course of action for material advancement – for earning money, expanding and establishing business, political success etc. This kind of intellect impels a person to engross himself in worldly tasks of all types and also to keep himself busy and make efficient utilization of his time. Research and development along with business activities in various fields of endeavour – food & agriculture, medicine, trade & commerce, law, politics, sociology, management, sports, music, arts – all belong to the realm of this intellect. Management philosophies, R & D patents of all types, legal codes etc. all are the products of the working of this type of intellect, which is termed *raajasik* by Bhagwadgita.

Taamsik Intellect

There is another basic variant of the intellect. Bhagwadgita calls it *taamsik*. This kind of intellect is the least refined and most banal, to put in crude words. It lacks the power of discrimination between moral and the immoral. Such an intellect weans a person away from activity and makes him lazy and indolent. Tendency to crime is also the result of the working of this intellect. Cunning, deceptive and corrupt are attributes of this type of intellect. Ignorance and confusion are the characteristic features of this intellect.

In practice, no person's intellect is purely *saatvik, raajasik* or *taamsik*. It is an admixture of the three elements which characterize intellect. Sometimes one element becomes predominant, on other occasions it is the other elements which hold sway.

Influences on Intellect

What is it that a person should do to ensure that his intellect remains pure and unsullied? Indeed, there are many factors which cast banal influences on the intellect or vitiate it in many other ways. Then what should you do to make sure that intellect does not become a hindrance in performance of right action for material and spiritual progress? The quality and complexion of your intellect depends upon past action, to a major extent. The types of *karma* that you have performed in your past or present life, have much to do to shape up your intellect. To have the right type of intellect with the right proportions of *saatvik, raajasik and taamasik* elements for the right occasion, pray to the Almighty God with devotion. He can put your intellect on the right track. Man is a creation of this Supreme Divinity or God and without His constant guidance and support, he cannot make real progress; he cannot achieve true happiness, success and what is known as self-realization. An agnostic may argue here that with his rational thinking, he doesn't need the concept of God to achieve success in life and to lead a happy life. But he does not realize that his intellect itself is sometimes not in his own control; it is subject to a myriad of influences through the spiritual media as a result of his own past actions. Therefore, he lives in a fool's paradise. The only solution of this problem is to have faith in the supreme Lord and keep communion with Him. He will put your intellect on the right path for fulfillment of your life's mission. Worship changes things and sometimes works where nothing else does.

Power of Prayer

Coming to the matter of worship, what do the human mortals pray to God for? What do they seek in this worship? To be candid, many among us pray to the Almighty God to solve our mundane problems – to help us tide over business crises, to cure our distressing illness or to fulfill our other material longings and desires. We pray at different places of worship, often seeking the fulfillment of our material desires. Since prayer to Almighty God is a powerful means of invoking His blessing, it works and man's desires are often fulfilled. But fulfillment of material desires cannot and doesn't bring lasting happiness. True happiness lies only in following God's commandments, His divine code of righteous conduct and action. Therefore pray to God to make your intellect follow the right path. If the intellect remains unsullied, the thinking process would remain rational and following the righteous code of action would become easier. So important is the role of intellect in our life.

The famous hymn of *Yajurveda* – the *Gayatri mantra* is devoted to the prayer to God for putting our intellect on the right course. Translated from the original Sanskrit into English, this hymn reads as follows:

"You are our Creator and Sustainer; we owe our life to you and look up to you to overcome our miseries; your great effulgence pervades the entire universe. We meditate on you and seek your blessings; Oh Lord! Direct our intellect on the righteous and virtuous path."

Here, it would be clear to you that most of the ordinary human beings cannot lead a hundred percent successful and happy life without being in communion with God and without invoking His divine blessing through prayer and worship.

ઉ

13. True Knowledge

It has been emphasized in the previous chapters that to lead a truly successful and happy life, you have to have a clear concept of the purpose of your existence in this world. Here, it is emphasized that successful living calls for true knowledge of man as a spiritual being, of the Almighty God, of the relationship between man and God, of laws of healthy living, of the doctrine of *karma* or divine retribution. True knowledge sets you on the path of real progress. Distorted knowledge would create obstacles in your progress. Wrong concepts, misplaced ideas and ill-conceived notions would effect wrong action and undermine peace and happiness. The previous twelve chapters of this book also constitute a humble little exposition of true knowledge. It is only through true knowledge that you can sail smoothly through the turbulent ocean of life with its ups and downs, successes and failures, pleasures and pains.

Knowledge Through Books

Which is this true knowledge we are talking about? Is it the knowledge gleaned through the books available on varied academic subjects – Arts, Science, Humanities, Engineering, Medicine or Commerce? There are so many subjects of study prescribed in the curricula of schools and colleges. You have Physics, Chemistry and Biology, you have Economics, Political Science, Geography, Accountancy and Languages; there are subjects on applied sciences – Electrical and Mechanical Engineering, Computer Science and then there are subjects related to Business and Commerce i.e. Business Management and Business Economics. There is a vast gamut of subjects related to modern Medicine and Surgery. And do not forget Psychology, Philosophy and allied sciences.

Incomplete Qualification

All the above fields of study and learning are for the purpose of occupation and livelihood. They are meant for churning out literates – graduates, post-graduates and doctorates from schools and colleges. These educational institutions create qualified persons for various professions for the purpose of enabling them to earn money. Today, information is often equated with knowledge. Knowledge is measured more in terms of bytes of information as is stored in the memory chips of computer hardware. But it is observed in many cases, that gross text book knowledge of fields of professional endeavour is unable to help mankind overcome his inherent frailties. It is found deficient in enabling a person to inculcate rational thinking, to understand the deeper truths of evolutionary life and to comprehend the philosophy of true human progress. No wonder, we find lot of confusion and misgiving in the civilized society of today. Literacy rates in most of the so called developed countries are well over 95 percent. People are educated and literate. But happiness and peace still eludes many of them. They run to Astrologers, Soothsayers and Spiritualists for assuaging their tension because they are always gripped by uncertainty and overwhelming concern about the future. Why are Yog and meditation centres becoming so popular in the affluent, developed countries of the West? The people find some solace, some enlightenment and some clear vision by pursuing these activities. They seek peace of mind more than money. The body can be gratified through money, the mind can also be gratified through the medium of wealth but the spirit in man can only be gratified through noble deeds and communion with God – the supreme spiritual entity.

Embedded in Spirituality

True knowledge is that which makes you a better human being; it gives you enlightenment and vision for the right, progressive action. True knowledge is the understanding of truth, fact and reality pervading the entire universe. It is a comprehension of the cause of all material and mundane phenomena – cause which is embedded in spirituality. Our sages and saints of the yore have always emphasized that the material world is changeable and perishable. Spiritual world is the ultimate reality, for, it is imperishable, immanent. Phenomena belonging to the realm of the spiritual world engender material phenomena and processes. But whereas matter is subject to ageing and changes, the spirit does not age nor dies. These are the facets of true knowledge which have to be assimilated by you for comprehension of the nature of divine elements working in the universe. This comprehension alone will enable you to conquer your weaknesses as a human being and realize your true potential for happy and successful living.

Cardinal Human Evils

Today you find most people indulging in a mad race for money. How many people truly know that greed is banal or that excessive lust for money shall erode their happiness and mental peace and would be an impediment to true progress? You have to know and realize that greed as an evil, is to be eschewed in practical life. Similarly with other cardinal human evils – anger, attachment, perverted ego and desire. By desire is meant unregulated sexual desire and indulgence. True knowledge alone is the precursor to proper action which brings about real progress. When we talk of real progress we mean comprehensive progress – material as well as spiritual.

Practise the Doctrine of Karma

The divine law of *karma* or 'cause and effect' must be understood. The ten facets of *dharma* or righteous action must be comprehended by each person who desires true happiness and fulfillment. True knowledge is available in religious scriptures. A wise man has to understand and apply this knowledge for his own betterment and for universal welfare. There should be no prejudices or preconceived notions in the study of the scriptures. The message of universal welfare contained in them must be adopted in practical life. Most sects and religious schools dwell upon one God; God is one but paths leading to Him are many. He understands all languages and is omniscient. It is irrational, rather ridiculous to create divides between peoples of different sects and cults. The world history is testimony to a lot of hatred, violence and bloodshed in the name of religion. Nothing could be more irreligious than this. All religious schools advocate love, selfless service and compassion. Disorder and disharmony in the world appears only when some sections of the population commit vicious and immoral acts out of sheer ignorance. Ignorance is a great curse.

Today we have many literates, many educated individuals but less learned and enlightened souls. Many an educated professional wants to earn more and more wealth for himself but shies away from charity. He also performs dishonest acts in his mad pursuit of wealth and in the process, undermines the welfare of his thousands of brethren. This action is also the result of ignorance or a lack of true knowledge.

It should be clearly understood that religion is not a mere school of thought or a mode of worship. It is a way of life. It covers in its vast ambit everything from the origin of man as a spiritual entity to the point of salvation – when the spiritual element of man through its evolutionary process, gets attuned with the supreme soul or God. Humanism lies at the core of religion.

True Knowledge – True Progress

The unfortunate thing is that, more often than not, concepts and definitions of right and the wrong, moral and immoral and virtue and vice are found to differ from person to person. This is also the result of ignorance or lack of true knowledge. Therefore, we all should endeavour to acquire true knowledge for our overall betterment and for universal welfare. We should realize that the entire world is one big family and each one of us is part of that family. Our actions should be such as will result in our individual development and promote the welfare of this vast family. Anything which affords you individual gain but is not conducive to family welfare, is improper, unrighteous and irreligious. The concept of true knowledge is not a philosophical hype. It is intended to help you to do your duty properly, to optimally utilize the time and other resources available with you and to make a 'success' of your life. Success here connotes the best performance of your duty and utilization of the short time in your limited life span. Whatever you do should help in forward mobility of your soul in its journey to its supreme abode. If you are a doctor, try to follow medical ethics scrupulously in your practice. Let sympathy and compassion be the key factors in your profession rather than the lust of money. If you are an Engineer, try to perform your duty without compromising with quality of your engineered products – never give in to that temptation for quick money through untoward means. If you are a journalist, do factual and honest reporting. Intellectual integrity is important in your working, whatever be your profession. In honest working lies the welfare of all.

The fields of education that train you for different trades or avocations constitute only a ground for acquisition of gross, material knowledge. True knowledge is that which is complete with its spiritual content. Realize that the material world is transitory but the spiritual realm is the eternal reality which rules all temporal phenomena. True knowledge acquired through proper education is that which does not nurture your ego. It is that which is conducive to welfare of all, not to 'survival of the fittest.' The concept of the survival of the fittest which has gained ground during the last and present century has bred grave inequality, tension, corruption, cut throat competition and malevolence in the human society. True knowledge makes you tolerant, accommodating and selfless. That is the reason why it forms such an important component of the divine code of righteous human conduct.

14. Adherence to Truth

You may start wondering why the stereotyped message of adherence to truth is sought to be given in this book. When the true human goal is happiness and contentment with universal well-being, this goal cannot be attained without adherence to truth. Falsehood is the evil that engenders enormous sorrow in this world. You know that human duties and rights are interrelated. One person's rights are protected in the other person's duties. The whole society functions smoothly and harmoniously only by virtue of the assiduous performance of human duties. Truth is an extremely important element of the performance of duties.

What does Truth Mean?

Fundamentally speaking, truth means absence of contradiction between what is seen and heard, felt and observed and experienced. Truthfulness or truthful conduct takes place when there is no mismatch between what is observed through senses and what is thought in the mind. The presence of truth implies the absence of illusion and delusion. Real human progress can be effected only through truthful conduct. It is said that a lie has no legs to stand upon. Indeed, untruth or falsehood is synonymous with instability, with disharmony. To hide one lie, you have to speak hundred lies. Falsehood produces a chain reaction of lies, of evil and sinful deeds. See how important truthfulness is as a code of conduct. No wonder, it rightfully finds a place in universal code of *dharma* or righteousness in Manusmriti.

Poisonous Lies

Every religious school of the world holds truth in high regard as a cardinal virtue in as much as truth has been equated with God. "Truth is God and God is truth", it has been said.

When you speak a lie to someone, it has two adverse effects; first, you experience a natural prick of conscience. Secondly, the other person feels extremely bad if he learns that he has been misled. You experience a surge of anger, hatred and contempt if you realize you have been deceived or duped by untruthful conduct. Often you feel dejected and sad. See how potent a poison untruth is. It creates many secondary vicious effects. The modern world of business is replete with truth defying contradictions. There is a tendency to hide the truth for extra monetary gains. The manufacturer who evades excise duty by false declaration of goods produced, the trader who evades import duty by under invoicing, the wholesaler who evades income tax by under declaration of income and the retailer who hoodwinks the buyer through exaggerated claims on the quality of his goods are all guilty of untruth. You can very well imagine how much good would accrue to the society if each person involved in business endeavoured to become truthful.

But it is not easy to adhere to truth. Where the entire atmosphere is vitiated, where everyone around appears to be indulging in underhand means to get things moving, truth suffers a great casualty because falsehood often becomes necessary for success. If deceit and falsehood become necessary for survival, values change and impropriety begins to be justified. When wrong doing in the society starts getting justified, it is a sure sign of regression and decay.

Speak and Live the Truth

Our enlightened forefathers have said, "Speak the truth and be polite". Truth spoken harshly is not desirable. But here you might ask "Truth is bitter, isn't it? " Yes, truth is often bitter but truth is not to be spoken harshly.

Truth spoken in a brash and impolite manner often defeats its very purpose. Diplomacy is regarded another great quality in modern age. Be diplomatic, but do not try to befool others through clever speech and manners. The heart should be pure and intentions clear. These days, diplomacy is held to be the manner and method of the clever conman. Diplomacy is intelligent speech and behaviour with clear intentions and honest outlook behind it. This is the ideal way to behave in the complex social environment of today.

Truth: A Powerful Virtue

Truth is such a powerful virtue that adherence to it washes away many vices. Take the case of Allan, a habitual flinger. Allan is an Advertising executive, in his mid-thirties. His profession exposes him to situations and persons of various shades. Though Allan is happily married, he is unable to resist the temptation of flings with persons interacting with him in the profession. Allan has been carrying on a clandestine affair with Tina, who does modelling assignments. The involvement is of such a type that Allan frequently returns home late at night.

Sometimes, he fails to return home even for the whole night. His irregular schedule has considerably upset his wife Susanne. But Allan has all along been pacifying her by ascribing his irregular schedule to the professional vagaries at his workplace. So he has been constantly lying to her and carrying on with his adulterous affair outside. What is the consequence of this kind of deceptive approach? First, it will vitiate Allan's own mind and intellect. Secondly, it will put Susanne into suspicion and strike a discordant note in their marital relationship. On one occasion, there is a strong altercation between husband and wife over this, which reinforces the suspicion carried by Susanne about Allan's

TRUTH

extra marital affair. This creates big tension at Allan's home which has markedly disturbed Allan's own mental peace. One day, Allan is advised by his close friend and peer Anderson to talk his heart out to his wife and not keep her in the dark about the affair. Now, Allan has been advised to be truthful to his wife. Imagine the effect of truthful conduct. If Allan is to speak truth to his wife, he can no longer continue his licentious ways because his marriage will be on the rocks. Following truthful conduct will prevent Allan from indulging in adulterous behaviour and would keep intact his marital and domestic harmony as also his own peace of mind. So truth is a double edged sword of virtue.

Truthfulness is the attribute of the innocent, of children whose minds are free from the polluting influence of the corrupt society. As the child grows into adulthood, he becomes increasingly subject to such influences and his truthfulness diminishes. The internationally famous Television films of USA – 'Superman', 'Superboy' and 'Superwoman' were all devoted to the 'destruction of evil' and 'pursuit of truth'. Truth is traditionally regarded as the fundamental virtue of civilized society but in modern times, unfortunately, this very virtue has received a jolt.

Truth and Justice

In the legal profession, truth is frequently suppressed or distorted. In a court of trial, the plaintiff, accused and the witness are asked to speak the truth, swearing by the name of God. But, if adherence to truth were so easy, there would be no crime, no litigation and no courts! The point emphasized here is that in the interest of peace, happiness and good of all, truthful conduct should be adopted as a deliberate choice. If a person sees the ultimate reality – God in everything, he would be naturally weaned from deceit and falsehood. Truthful conduct is synonymous with honesty. In chapter 9 of this book, a detailed account was provided of the significance of honesty for happy and successful living. Truth and honesty are complementary elements, faces of the same coin. But truth, in as far as it is stated to be an element of the universal righteous code of conduct, really pertains to purity of action, which is devoid of falsehood and deceit.

Truth and Virtues

Mahatma Gandhi, the famous saint-reformer of modern India, is remembered internationally sixty-five years after his death for his two great qualities – adherence to truth and practice of non-violence. Truth covers in its vast ambit a great number of virtues. It makes man humble, honest and forbearing. It is the seed of many noble human qualities that have sustained human welfare through the course of the world's tumultuous history.

Truth: The Practical Aspect

In some practical situations, it becomes difficult to speak the truth. Such situations may arise in domestic or professional or social life. For example, your dear brother has met with a serious accident and is struggling for his life in the hospital. You wish to convey this to his wife who is on a professional tour abroad. How will you inform her? Would you straightaway speak the entire truth? Consider another situation. Your small son out of innocent curiousity asks you questions about sex or how he was born, which are embarrassing for you. You consider it improper to tell him everything at this tender age. Again you have to satisfy him with an answer which would be away from truth. If you are a lawyer, you have to defend your client whether or not he is on the right side of truth. Practical constraints of professional life may compel you to fight for untruth, although this kind of conduct is not sanctioned by the scriptures.

Think Before You Speak

In all those situations, where you have to take recourse to untruth because of circumstantial compulsions, take care to speak those words which are conducive to the welfare of all. In those cases where truthful speech prejudices anybody's interests, refrain from it. Think before you speak. Your words are important instruments of behaviour and action which will have bearing on the welfare of those you are interacting with.

These days, persons who mean what they say and say what they mean – the true simpletons are few. Frequently, people take pride in befooling others through mischievous lies or for fulfilling their selfish narrow ends. Especially this appears to be true of many of those in politics. Many politicians are adept in the art of hoodwinking the masses. They will swear by the people before elections to work for their welfare and after winning the elections, callously ignore the interests of their voters.

To all those of us who desire success and true happiness, it should be clear that truthfulness, as a code of conduct, needs to be scrupulously followed in all our actions. Given the inherent contradictions of modern social, political, economic and professional institutions, adherence to truth is indeed like treading the proverbial sword's edge. But once a person realises that through truthful conduct, he would be a long term gainer, truthfulness becomes a part of his character.

15. Mind and Its Regulation

Mind is the gateway to the world. It is the vehicle for every human activity. It is the medium of thought, seat of emotions and the driver of all impulses. It is verily the most important entity in the human being. Nothing is possible to achieve in the world without fixation and regulation of mind in the performance of the requisite tasks. Sages, savants, scholars, philosophers, psychologists, physicians all agree on the singularly important role of mind in civilized human existence. Successful accomplishment of any mundane work calls for knowledge, skills and concentration which are acquired through mind. If the secret of success is the proper functioning of the mind, then surely the mind holds the key to happiness, bliss and salvation of the human being.

Mind and Mental Phenomena

There is an old saying in native Punjabi which translates as "Vanquish the mind and vanquish the world; defeated by mind is defeated by the world." A lot of study and research has gone into the subject of mind and mental phenomena like perception, emotions, telepathy, dreams, intuition, emotion and clairvoyance. Psychology and Psychoanalysis are the branches of professional learning that deal with the subject of mind. But it has to be admitted that our understanding of the entity called 'mind' is very limited and deficient. If a person is mentally deranged, he is unfit for the society and a burden on others. However a normal person who is well educated, highly skilled and physically healthy but of an unstable mind is also more of a liability than an asset for the society. His sterling qualities are of no use to his community if he suffers from mental aberrations like mania, depression or schizophrenia.

In various chapters of this book, the cardinal issues that influence happiness and success of civilized human beings have been individually discussed. The action points – dos and don'ts underlying these issues have a common denominator, which is the human mind. The errant, ever excitable mind has to be brought under control for every successful action to be performed. Control of the mind, therefore, is the cornerstone of all successful actions.

Constitution of Mind

How do we bring the mind under control? To answer this question, we have to understand the constitution of the mind. The mind is a material entity. Material means made of matter and the latter consists of the five principal elements – earth, fire, water, space and wind. Matter actually consists of electrons, protons, neutrons and positrons which are its building units. These particles combine to form atoms and molecules. Definitely, mind is also some combination of one or more of these particles or their subparticles. Material entities can be modified by material means. Hence, to shape the mind, we need to exercise material influence. Our scholars of the yore, accomplished in yoga, taught us that to control our mind, we need to regulate our diet. We need to work on our diet such that the quantity and quality of food that we eat produces more of beneficial and less of baneful effects on the mind. Food eaten in accordance with one's physical constitution will increase strength and stability of the mind. Food taken in moderate quantities will have a similar effect. The role of the food in influencing the mind needs a more elaborate explanation. There are seven types of physical constitution (*prakriti*) according to the classical Aayurvedic School of medicine. These are enumerated below.

1. *Kaph prakriti*
2. *Pitt prakriti*
3. *Vaat prakriti*
4. *Kaph - Pitt prakriti*
5. *Pitt - Vaat prakriti*
6. *Kaph - Vaat prakriti*
7. *Kaph - Pitt - Vaat prakriti*

The Three Basic Elements

Here *Kaph, Pitt* and *Vaat* denote the three basic elements (phlegm, bile and air respectively) which regulate our body processes and functions. Every item of our food has specific characteristics in that it is either *kaph* vitiating, *pitt* vitiating or *vaat* vitiating. Similarly, food items could be *kaph* balancing, *pitt* balancing or *vaat* balancing. The balanced condition of *kaph, pitt* and *vaat* is the condition of sound health. One should select such food as is compatible with one's *prakriti* so that the three elements remain in an optimum or balanced condition. This is the condition of good health which actually means a healthy mind in a healthy body.

Breath Effect

The other but more important factor influencing mental health is our technique of breathing. It is very easy for anyone to observe that the lengths of the inhaled and exhaled breath are equal when one is in a normal condition of mind. But during tension and stress, the exhaled breath is longer than the inhaled breath. In a state of worry, fear or anger, the same phenomenon can be experienced. Thus to de-stress oneself, one needs to voluntarily correct one's breathing cycle by equalizing the lengths of the inhaled breath and exhaled breath. The *vaat* (air) element of our system has a direct and profound effect on the mind. Deep breathing and matched intake and outflow of air has a soothing and beneficial effect on the mind. Praanaayaam or breath-exercise has been the recommended and established way to bring the excitable, unstable and errant mind in one's control.

The Required Posture

The third and equally important factor in maintaining mental health is one's posture. Aayurvedic science says that vitiation of *vaat* element is the result of wrong physical posture apart from other factors. The *vaat* (air) element vitiated, in turn, vitiates the mind. A mind which is irritated by an unbalanced *vaat* becomes wavering, loses focus.

Prayer: Divine Interventional Tool

The above paragraphs touched upon the material influences on the material entity that mind is. But now we come back to the all pervading, eternal control of the universal spiritual entity called 'God' on the human mind. God is omniscient and omnipotent. Nothing in the material nature is outside his control. Hence, God as the creator of mind, is its complete master and possesses full control over it. That is why, the primordial scriptures – Vedas are eloquent on the prayers to the almighty God by his human subjects seeking his ennobling influence over their minds. A man praying to God to achieve stability, serenity or composure of the mind at once puts in action the process of the benevolent God imparting such positive attributes to the mind.

A prayer to God who is the supreme creator and benefactor of his human subjects is, therefore, the divine interventional tool to bring stability and composure to the mind. Nothing is easy for the person with an unstable, errant, weak and ignoble mind and no task is too difficult for the person whose mind is stable, calm, strong and noble. But to achieve stability, equanimity and strength of the mind, a person needs to achieve detachment from the material world and, at the same time, perform extensive practice of mind control. The ways to do this practice have already been elaborated upon in the foregoing paragraphs.

Structure of Mind

Many philosophers and thinkers have written treatises on ancient Hindu scriptures dealing with the subject of mind control. Mind is a great vehicle of thought, action and speech and is, therefore, the prime subject in the context of human development. Whether you are doing physical work or mental work for avocation, a focussed mind and concentrated attention are essential for efficiency and professional success. The mind itself is required to be trained for achieving concentration and focus.

Here it would be relevant to provide an exposition of the structure of the mind. The mind consists of two portions – a conscious mind and a subconscious portion. The conscious mind is what we use in our day-to-day existence but it constitutes only the ten percent of the entire mind. Ninety percent of the mind is the subconscious mind. The subconscious mind is an extremely powerful element and is the storehouse of impressions, knowledge and learning. The conscious mind is the active, in-use portion of the mind but the subconscious portion obviously has a much larger expanse and purview and it exercises covert control over the conscious portion. In fact, the subconscious and conscious minds are like portions of a piece of ice floating over water. The portion sticking outside the water surface constitutes ten percent of the whole piece, whereas the portion immersed in water constitutes ninety percent of the piece of ice. The conscious mind is comparable to the more visible portion of the piece of ice. It is what is apparent and what we use in our daily life. Memory, perception, intuition and meditation are subjects of the subconscious mind. Mental training and practice of mind control referred to in the previous lines, really belong to the realm of subconscious mind. Invocation of divine powers through prayer strengthens and enriches the subconscious mind.

It may be observed through the above discussion that the entire process of mental training and mind control is scientific. In fact the working of the corporeal body, the mind, the intellect, the soul and the supreme soul is also scientific because they follow set predefined principles enshrined in our prime scriptures.

The mind is central to the existence of man. This is even borne out by the etymology of the word 'mind' which is similar to that of the word 'man'. Man thinks through the mind, acts and works through his mind and feels through the mind. Hence, mind control is of great importance.

Mind: Epicentre of Consciousness

The above exposition of the mind has nothing to do with the traditionally understood subject of religion. This exposition revolves around the scientific understanding of metaphysical truths evidenced by logic and rationality. Psychologists and parapsychologists have discovered through extensive research that mind is the epicenter of consciousness and this is in agreement with scriptural knowledge. A Western philosopher had remarked, "Imagination rules the world." How you fix up ideas, desires, objectives, ambitions or aspirations in your mind shapes up the mind and its tendencies which, in turn, shape up your actions in the direction of your goals and objectives.

While on the subject of mind and mind control, it would be necessary to provide a detailed account of the practical techniques of mind control through regulation of breath, called Praanaayaam. There is abundance of literature on this subject. But an attempt shall be made in the following paragraphs to provide a clear and concise treatment of the techniques of Praanaayaam that can be understood and regularly practised by the common folks.

What is Praanaayaam?

The word Praanaayaam means regulation or control of the breath. *'Praan'* is the vital wind energy element that sustains our life. The continuous cycle of inhalation and exhalation of air is the manifestation of this vital natural energy that living beings are endowed with. Deliberate regulation of this natural breathing cycle is what *Praanaayaam* is all about. The *Praans* are of five types – *Praan Vaayu, Apaan Vaayu, Samaan Vaayu, Byan Vaayu* and *Udan Vaayu.* Whereas the *Praan Vaayu* functions through intake and outflow of air through our nostrils, the *Apaan Vaayu* works to expel urine and stool from our body. Likewise, other

types of *vaayu* perform different functions in our body. The *Praan Vaayu* possesses control over body functions from the thoracic region upwards towards the head. The *Apaan Vaayu* resides in the abdominal region and similarly carries out the work of elimination of waste material from our intestines and urinary organs. The important matter to understand is that *Praan Vaayu* is connected to all other types of *vaayu*. Further, all these five *vaayu*-elements are connected to the human mind. The mind works through these *vaayu* elements. Changes in the disposition of the mind are reflected in the changes in working patterns of these five types of *vaayu*. As already mentioned before in this chapter, the mind is subtle but a material entity and, therefore, can be controlled through material means based on the five elements of nature – air, earth, water, fire and space. Mind control through *praanaayaam* makes use of the air element of nature for influencing the mind. Our ancient practitioners of *yog* had prescribed various types of *praanaayaams*. Of these, five most important ones are described here. Their stated importance is based on the fact that they are easiest to learn and practise by ordinary folks. These *praanaayaams* are elaborated below.

1. **Kapaalbhaati** – This *praanaayaam* involves rhythmic inward movements of abdomen coinciding with jerky exhalation strokes. The abdominal and exhalation strokes may be performed at the rate of 40 to 60 strokes per minute. This exercise regulates the functioning of *praan vayu and apaaan vaayu*. It tones the intestines, at the same time conditioning the flow of *praan vaayu* for better intake of vital air. This *praanayaam* tones up indirectly all the abdominal organs. It helps to make the bowel moments regular. Better intake of *praan vaayu* and regulation of *apaan vayu* improves blood circulation and provides a characteristic glow to the face. Hence, the name Kapaalbhaati (literally meaning a brilliant face).

2. **Anulom–Vilom Praanaayaam** – This *praanaayaam* involves slow deep inhalation through one nostril and exhalation at the same rate through the other nostril. This process of inhalation followed by exhalation alternately through each nostril is continuously performed till one gets half tired. At this point, the inhalation – exhalation activity is stopped for about two minutes during which normal breathing is done. The standard time for one inhalation breath or one exhalation breath is 2½ seconds. This exercise normalizes the *kaph* and *pitt* elements in the body and is, therefore, beneficial for overall physical and mental health. It improves mental stability and concentration.

3. **Bhastrika Praanaayaam** – This *praanaayaam* is performed by taking a slow, deep inhalation breath followed by a jerky, short and forceful exhalation. This *praanaayaam* also improves the balance of the three *doshas* in the portion of the body above the neck. Restoration of the balance of *vaat* provides strength and stability to the mind. A mind, which is strong and stable is obviously not erratic and does not wander. It remains calm and lends a composed disposition to a person. An excitable and errant mind makes a person go astray in action and this *praanaayaam* serves to correct exactly this.

4. **Bhraamari Praanaayaam** – This *praanaayaam* is performed by closing the ears by tips of the thumbs, closing the eyes, placing the index fingers over forehead and then taking a deep breath and holding the breath. While holding the breath, eyes are gently covered by fingers. During the process, after the intake of breath and closing the nostrils by pressing from outside, a humming sound is produced for half a minute. This humming sound resembles the sound

produced by a wasp. This *praanaayaam* also tones up the facials organs i.e. nose, eyes and ears. It regulates the *praan vaayu* residing in this part of the body and has a soothing and calming effect on the mind.

Almighty God

Regular practice of the above *praanaayaam* techniques is greatly helpful in control of the ever excitable, errant mind. Finally, an exposition will be provided of the profound influence that the Almighty universal spirit has over the mind as this all pervading spirit has control over all material entities of the nature. You may call this universal spirit the Almighty God or give it any other name. This spirit is the Creator, Controller, Sustainer and Destroyer of the entire material world. Prayer to the benevolent God for providing beneficial conditioning of the mind has been spelt out in the ancient scriptures – the Vedas. Certain hymns of Yajurved are devoted to the direct prayer to God for making our minds strong, stable and calm enable them to absorb beneficent energy from Him.

This prayer is purely scientific because God exists as spiritual energy with complete power and control over material world.

Mind is the fulcrum of human existence. It is crucial to human activities, accomplishments, emotions and success. It is truly the gateway to happiness and sorrow and all other contrasting emotional states. If a person has learnt to train the mind and exercise control over it and, at the same, time learnt to tap the divine spiritual energy pervading the universe for refining and purifying the mind, no task or target is too difficult for him. He acquires the key to all riches of the mundane as well as the spiritual world.

16. Abiding Faith

A western philosopher had remarked – "If there were no God, it would be necessary to invent Him". Man is characterized by limited knowledge, intelligence, physical strength and a limited life span. So is the case with other living beings. Basic metaphysical truths expounded in the Vedas provide a clear insight into three prime entities in the vast universe. These are matter, living beings (souls) and a universal soul or God. Attributes of these three entities and their interrelationship is the universalistic knowledge, which forms the foundation of human existence on this globe. However, most of the human beings while having faith in the existence of a supernatural power, do not base this faith on rational, scientific precepts of Vedas – the most ancient scriptures.

The Higher Divine Power

The very manner in which human beings exist in this world, the way in which they seek to fulfill their aspirations and desires along with the experiences that they gather in the process naturally make them seek the help of a higher divine power – a supreme creator and sustainer, who will overcome their misery and sorrow and help them achieve their material goals. This natural leaning or dependence actually stems from the basic limitations of physical, intellectual and mental capacity of man. This dependence also gets reinforced by the natural feeling in the mind of man about his small and inconsequential size in this vast, infinite universe. Thus, faith in God as the creator comes naturally and instinctively to man. True, there are many persons among the human population who are agnostics. They discount and dismiss the existence of any

God. But their numbers have always been few. There goes a story of a hard rationalist who loudly refuted the existence of any God. He put up a billboard outside his house which declared **'God is nowhere'**. When that man died, people were surprised to see that the same billboard read **'God is now here'.** Eventually, before his death, the hard agnostic had split the word **'nowhere'** into two separate words **'now here'** on his billboard.

Faith: Action and Effect

Logic or rationality is the cornerstone of mundane human life. A person acts in a certain manner because he thinks that his action would have an effect that he desires. There may or may not be an evidence or hard proof of the belief in this action and effect. But he has faith that his action would result in a certain and desired effect. Mentally, man is conditioned to think and behave in a logical manner. Even an insane person goes by what he thinks is logical. Thus, rationality is at the bottom of all human thinking and, therefore, also at the bottom of all human actions. The intellect in man is inherently designed to work in this way. In this conditioned setting, man seeks the help of a supreme creator, a supernatural power to resolve his life problems and fulfill his aspirations and longings. He connects himself with that supernatural power through demonstrated obeisance and prayer. Thus are invented various types of imaginary Gods and Goddesses. You will find numerous types of deities and modes of worship prevailing in the world. The basic understanding and philosophy underlying the phenomenon is common.

Faith and Intellect

The issue of faith in a supernatural power called God, therefore, settles in human mind naturally through observation and experience. But human intellect is also of different grades. Not all human beings possess the same type of intellect. Some are very

गीता
पुराण

sharp in understanding and comprehension. Others are relatively dull. Some others are labeled as hard of understanding and 'dunce' or 'duffers'. Intellect is the faculty of discriminating between right and the wrong, between truth and untruth. Since the quality of this intellect and its discerning and discriminating power differs so widely from person to person, there has to be some pool of perfect knowledge through which the working of this hugely populated earth can be regulated. If all logical considerations point to the existence of a creator, sustainer and regulator God, then there must be available to His human subjects His divine knowledge as a guide to successful human living. Verily and truly, this knowledge is available. God exists and so does His divine knowledge in all ages and times. This divine knowledge is enshrined in the four Vedas (Rigved, Yagurved, Saamaved and Atharvaved). These scriptures are primordial and timeless. Hence, they are immutable too, being of divine origin. All branches of worldly knowledge prevailing today have roots in Vedas. This fundamental truth has to be comprehended by the seeker of true knowledge and happiness and success. This is a core truth which is self evident and needs no crutches of manmade material evidence to stand upon. This truth is proof up on its own like the brilliant sun and the distant twinkling stars.

Success: Efforts and Fortune

Man's success in the world depends upon various factors as has already been outlined in chapter 7th of this small book. Based on what has been stated in the said chapters, it can be inferred that success in any activity calls for proper efforts and good fortune. Both efforts and fortune can be influenced by tapping the divine energy of the Supreme Spirit called God. The Vedas are clear and eloquent on this issue. Through prayer and meditation, a human being is able to influence his mind, body and intellect beneficially. He acquires stability, focus and strength of the mind.

He is able to refine and sharpen his intellect and through better understanding of the laws of good health, he is able to improve his physical health and endurance too. These multifarious benefits give a person head on advantage in pursuit of his goals. "Prayer changes things", it is said. People generally believe that prayer works through faith and that faith could even be blind. But true faith is not blind. It is based on rational, scientific considerations. Science is systematic knowledge borne out by standing proofs and testimonies. Hence, it is true knowledge. Vedas are the repositories of true knowledge and the concepts of prayer and meditation have only to be applied and adopted by the success hungry man of the twenty-first century. He has to understand, that the entire universe functions scientifically and hence logically and rationally, for, scientific approach, logic and rationality are nearly synonymous terms.

Prayer and Happiness

The power of faith in changing situations and events truly comes from the universal spiritual energy called God. The supreme creator has declared in Vedas that man has been created for leading a happy healthy life of at least a hundred years on this earth. He has not created man to live in suffering, poverty, disease or destitution. For Him, human subjects are meant to follow the principles and precepts laid down in the Vedas and live happily and successfully. God is the fountainhead of all positive energy. He is a vast, infinite ocean of bliss. This nectar of divine happiness or bliss actually flows from Him to His human subjects during the course of human meditation upon God. This divine nectar of happiness and knowledge has the power to purify human mind and intellect. If mind and intellect are purified then man becomes fully equipped to take on the challenges of life and come out victorious. Further, there is something called luck or fortune. The theory of *karma* stipulates that good actions attract good results. Bad actions i.e. immoral, sinful and unrighteous actions invite retribution in the form of sorrows and miseries. Actually prayer has even the power to destroy misfortune by deferring the inevitable fruit of bad *karma* or by making the human subject mentally steadfast to endure the retribution of bad *karma*. Either way, prayer to the Almighty and meditation upon him opens the floodgates to happiness and success.

Faith in the supernatural benevolent power is demonstrated by people in various ways. Most of the schools of religion essentially agree on the existence of an omnipresent, omniscient and omnipotent God. Prayer gives us clarity of ideas; it provides stability to the mind and makes us more optimistic and energetic in the pursuit of our goals. People – young, middle-aged and old, across a spectrum of castes, creeds, races and nationalities are privy to the demonstrated power of faith in the supernatural in their individual lives. This power works, because it is real.

Prayer does Help

Prayer as an action based on abiding faith can help you to steer the ship of your life through the turbulent ocean of the world. Prayer provides you the fortitude of mind to endure adversity. Prayer helps you to overcome your vanity which is a big impediment to progress. Prayer makes you just and levelheaded because the Almighty God who is the object of your prayer is an embodiment of justice. Therefore, rather than being an agnostic, understand the scientific and rational basis of existence of God and the power of prayer to God.

An exposition of the subject of faith would remain incomplete if the matter of blind faith remains untouched. By dictionary definition, faith is a belief borne out or not borne out by logic. Faith not borne out by logic or reasoning, is blind faith. Blind faith is superstition. The divine scriptures, Vedas declare that whereas

God is omniscient, man is not all knowing. Man has very limited intellect, knowledge and understanding. Therefore, it is natural and likely that human beings conceptualize God in different ways. Since God is not a subject of the physical world perceived by human senses, different persons develop different ideas about the nature and attributes of God. Among these human beings, there are also some who are`total agnostics. Some people make images, totems and idols of God while others see him as formless. There are, accordingly, multiple modes of worship. While on this subject, it would be relevant to mention that there are some religious schools which do not talk of any God and merely refer to an immutable law of cause and effect. The human race, at the same time has been witness to lot of conflicts, wars and destruction in the name of religion or because of differing religious beliefs.

Understanding Metaphysical Truths

No human being naturally wants or likes conflict, tension, disharmony, violence, pain and suffering. But history is testimony to violent conflicts in the name of religion. This only shows that human individuals' knowledge and understanding about metaphysical truths has not been complete and clear. That is the reason for multiple faiths and modes of worship. And this is precisely because of the fact that human beings are inherently limited of intelligence, knowledge and intellectual application. That is why the creator, in his infinite wisdom, has handed down his divine knowledge to humanity in the form of Vedas. The knowledge enshrined in Vedas is universalistic and broad based. This knowledge is true knowledge of nature, God, living beings and their interrelation. This is the knowledge with which humanity is supposed to live in perfect peace and harmony. This is the knowledge to apply even for development of implements and tools of material science without degrading the environment. This is the knowledge which is required to the used by human beings for communion with the creator and for deriving strength, wisdom and superior energy for leading a better life. This is the knowledge to be applied by individual human beings for achieving success in their endeavours. This is the knowledge whose application can establish total peace and happiness. This is the knowledge which educates and enlightens a man on true faith which is founded on logic and this is verily the knowledge which shows how human beings will connect themselves to God – their creator, preceptor and sustainer. Thus, abiding faith in God with which are related worship, prayer and meditation needs to be rational and scientific to be beneficial for human beings. Irrational and blind faith would lead to imperfect or no communion with the divine energy called God. Blind faith leading to superstitions would result in disharmony, tensions, sorrow, miseries. We all have been created by the Almighty God. He alone knows what is good for us. We must follow, in our best wisdom, His injunctions spelt out in His scriptures – the Vedas. That is indeed the cornerstone of happy, healthy and successful living.

17. Collective Existence

Since time immemorial, human beings have lived on this planet earth in huge numbers inhabiting almost the entire landmass of the earth. In their collective existence, they have lived as groups, communities, societies and nations. At different places on the earth, there are gross and finer variations in climate patterns, flora and fauna as also variations among the human beings in terms of colour of skin, facial features and even mental traits. These variations are often termed as racial differences. Because of these differences and environmental variations as mentioned above, humans have always lived during the course of history as different nations. The concept of nation state in fact, is not invented by man. It is nature or God ordained. The fundamental scriptures – Vedas bring out very clearly the concept of nation state. The scriptures also dwell at length upon the systems required to be put in place to run these nation states smoothly and also to enable these nation states co-exist harmoniously and peacefully.

Happiness in a Collective Setting

An account of the different elements of peaceful and happy human existence at the individual level and in the context of individual interactions is provided in the previous chapters of the book. However, individual human happiness is influenced not only by other human beings as individuals but collectively by communities, societies and nations too. A person who follows scrupulously the tenets of righteousness and religiosity but lives in a community of morally semi-debased persons can never exist peacefully. Further, the code of moral conduct or 'dharma' applying to communities and nations must also be followed for these communities and nations to co-exist peacefully. Hence the systems of governance, laws and codes of civil society, international laws etc. also attain overriding importance in this context.

Today's world is a classic example illustrating the statements made above. Many nations in the twenty-first century world are witness to the internal incidence of crime, corruption, social unrest, income disparity, violence and insurgency. This situation exists in spite of prevailing laws, codes, rules and systems of administration. The citizens live in deep mistrust of the governments. This situation is far from ideal.

The Global Scenario

The year 2011 has seen many regimes in populous countries of the African continent under attack by their own citizens who took to streets defying the law and order enforcing machinery. Libya and Egypt showed this popular unrest demonstrating the government – public mistrust in a glaring manner. In India, the recent episodes of scams and scandals of economic malfeasance by politicians or bureaucrats is another example. In India, and much more so in Pakistan, the episodes of insurgency and terrorist violence occurring on an almost regular basis are pointers at serious issues of disaffection between governments and citizens. All these phenomena show that collective existence of human beings needs to be regulated by systems that will actually establish peace and harmony on a sustainable basis. In other words, there are serious lacunae and shortcomings in the existing systems. What are these shortcomings?

Systems for Healthy Existence

In the previous chapter, it has been mentioned that every human being has limited mental ability and knowledge. Hence he has limited faculty of understanding and analyzing. Because of this reason, manmade rules, codes and systems can never be perfect and foolproof. They are constantly refined, modified and fine

tuned as seen in practice because of experiences warranting such action. Hence the need to adopt God ordained systems for human institutions. These systems are written down in Vedas and Manusmriti and need to be applied in our formal groups, communities and nations. Furthermore, the code of international interaction in regard to trade, commerce, defense, warfare, environment, aviation, tourism, etc. also needs to be taken out from these divine scriptures. Problems besetting mankind would be speedily resolved when these systems are in place. These core truths have to be understood and applied by the tension ridden and confused generation of today. The sooner these are understood, the better it is. I would like to reiterate the premise behind this assertion – these systems based on Vedas and Manusmriti would come directly from the creator who alone knows best what is good for His subjects. So this presumption has to be at the basis of what we do to formulate systems for our healthy existence.

Faith: Rational and Scientific Basis

The present generation believes and wrongly so that civilized human existence is about 4000 years old. Historians, Paleontologists, Zoologists etc. at present neither have the tools nor the wherewithal to trace the past span of civilized human existence. They go by observations and conjectures and assumptions. You cannot expect any better than this, because human beings are innately of limited intelligence and vision. Here comes the question of faith in a divine creator and his knowledge on a rational and scientific basis. We glean through the pages of our scriptures and epics and understand that civilized human existence is millions of years old and predates even that in a time continuum that follows a cyclic pattern. We find that utopia existed during the reign of Yudhishthir (about 5000 years ago) and during the period of Sri Rama (about 1200,000 years ago). We find accounts in recorded and unrecorded history, of regimes in which there was perfect moral order, complete compliance with civil laws and accordingly, perfect peace and harmony in the society. What I intend to convey in these sentences is that such peace and harmony was the result of adherence to Vedic code of law in human society. Manusmiriti, the mundane code of living is based on Vedas in fundamental terms. Hence we as rational, scientific and enlightened human beings ought to realize this core truth and adopt the systems enshrined in these scriptures in our social and political institutions. Global peace and harmony would not remain a distant dream then.

To conclude this chapter, individual human happiness and systems of regulation of human institutions are interrelated. These systems have to be rational, scientific, and above all, based on Vedas and Manusmriti, which contain the divine code of human existence, to be useful in the true sense. Based on the fundamental premise that man owes his existence to a supreme divine Creator and so man owes even his peaceful and happy existence to the same Creator, man has to apply the divine injunctions of these scriptures for peace, happiness, success and self-actualization.

Epilogue

The world is constantly on the move. Nothing is static, for, time never stands still. The human individual is not a puppet in the hands of Almighty Creator, as many might be led into believing. Man in his own right is a divine entity. His potentialities are great. The divine, spiritual element in him has the power to take him to dizzy heights of material glory. It is upto the intelligent person to imbibe the right knowledge for this purpose and adopt it in his own life. Discipline of the mind holds the key to accomplishment of all worldly tasks. It is also essential for development of spirit which leads to true fulfillment of human life. Let each one of us, in all his wisdom, endeavour to grasp true knowledge and train his mind to work in the direction of true progress which is conducive to universal welfare more than the success and happiness of his own self.

POPULAR SCIENCE

9496 A • Rs. 120/-

2215 S • ₹ 150/-
Available in Hindi also.

2214 S • ₹ 150/-
Available in Hindi also.

Set Code: 4514 S

- Over 900 Illustrations
- Over 800 Pages
- 890 Articles
- Four Volumes

FREE
Buy all 4 Vols. & get 5th Volume free with an Audio-Video DVD worth ₹135/-

Set 4 Vols.: ₹ 780/-
Each Vol.: ₹ 195/-

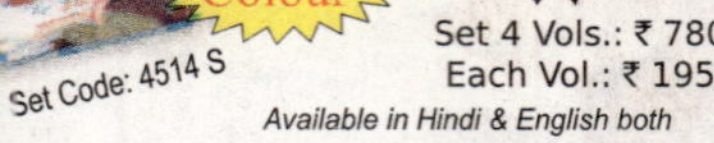

Available in Hindi & English both

8716 T • ₹ 160/-

HC009 • ₹ 620/-

HC008 • ₹ 399/-

HC005 • ₹ 540/-

This Library is must for every student of a School or a College

Also equally useful for everyone else

Price: ₹ 600/-

Contains 4 books of ₹ 150/- each

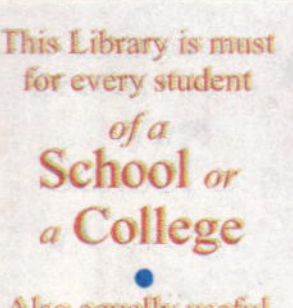

8702 B• ₹ 150/-

6678 D • ₹ 195/-

6679 A • ₹ 150/-

9660 K • ₹ 250/-

4 Books of the Library

₹ 150/- Page 256 (with CD) English Conversation
₹ 150/- Page 310 Grammar & Punctuation
₹ 150/- Page 316 How to use English
₹ 150/- Page 344 English Vocabulary

QUIZ BOOKS

8965 D • ₹ 150/-

7726 K • ₹ 120/-

7727 L • ₹ 120/-

7723 F • ₹ 100/-

9412 C • ₹ 120/-

7753 G • ₹ 100/-

7725 B • ₹ 100/-

7722 E • ₹ 100/-

GENERAL BOOKS

9532 D • ₹ 250/- HB

8526 B • ₹ 125/-

8712 M • ₹ 150/-

8711 K • ₹ 195/

9821 K • ₹ 175/-

9699 T • ₹ 100/-

9767 B • ₹ 150/-

5114 B • ₹ 88/

4175 A • ₹ 135/-

9459 H • ₹ 1000/- (HB)

9041 A • ₹ 195/-

4022 D • ₹ 100

SELF-IMPROVEMENT

New

698 R • ₹ 195/-

9498 C • ₹ 180/-

9490 H • ₹ 175/-

5464 R • ₹ 80/-

9096 B • ₹ 120/-

5614 E • ₹ 150/-

4008 J • ₹ 120/-

9026 D • ₹ 120/-

9786 M • ₹ 195/-

491 J • ₹ 100/-

8885 D • ₹ 80/-

9081 D • ₹ 150/-

9091 E • ₹ 120/-

9060 B • ₹ 120/-

9684 F • ₹ 195/-

8928 D • ₹ 80/-

9449 A • ₹ 195/-

9788 R • ₹ 195/-

MANAGEMENT/JOB/CARRIER/BUSINESS & PROFESSION

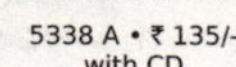

9461 K • ₹ 135/-

5338 A • ₹ 135/- with CD

8979 A • ₹ 120/-

9405 B • ₹ 150/-

5441 D • ₹ 195/-

8883 D • ₹ 120/-

9672 G • ₹ 150/-

9682 D • ₹ 120/-

New

9697 P • ₹ 195/-

9313 D • ₹ 150/-

5623 B • ₹ 195/-

9439 L • ₹ 150/-

4005 E • ₹ 150/-

5643 B • ₹ 120/-

9431 C • ₹ 175/-

8990 C • ₹ 96/-

4018 D • ₹ 150/-

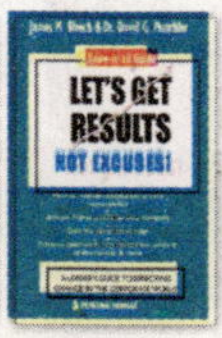

9079 B • ₹ 195/-

5618 D • ₹ 120/-

5640 C • ₹ 120/-

5615 D • ₹ 150/-

8972 C • ₹ 80/-

4001 A • ₹ 150/-

5646 A • ₹ 225/-

4017 D • ₹ 120/-

PERSONALITY DEVELOPMENT

9670 E • ₹ 240/-

9678 R • ₹ 195/-

9450 B • ₹ 195/-

9487 E • ₹ 150/-

9466 T • ₹ 96/-

5639 B • ₹ 80/-

5641 A • ₹ 150/-

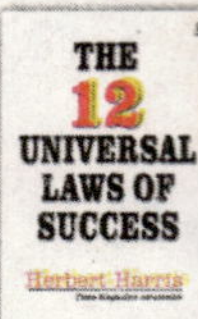

9088 C • ₹ 195

9667 B • ₹ 150/-

9666 A • ₹ 150/-

9696 M • ₹ 220/-

9973 B • ₹ 110/-

9981 B • ₹ 96/-

8868 D • ₹ 120/-

8966 E • ₹ 100/-

9070 B • ₹ 195/-

9028 D • ₹ 140

STUDENT DEVELOPMENT

9090 A • ₹ 195/-

9668 C • ₹ 150/-

9071 D • ₹ 140/-

9455 C • ₹ 150/-

5622 A • ₹ 120/-

9967 C • ₹ 120/-

2241 J • ₹ 100/- H

94441 S • ₹ 195/-

9654 D • ₹ 100/

9652 D • ₹ 120/-

8962 A • ₹ 100/-

9089 D • ₹ 135/-

4016 D • ₹ 160/-

4009 K • ₹ 110/- H

8997 B • ₹ 120/-

4010 L • ₹ 100/- H

9787 P • ₹ 100/-

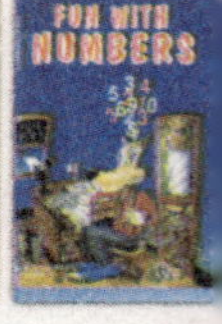

2244 D • ₹ 80/-

SAYING/QUOTATIONS/PROVERBS

9474 F • ₹ 170/-

9789 A • ₹ 150/-

9953 A • ₹ 100/-

8947 E • ₹ 100/-

8999 D • ₹ 80/-

5512 A • ₹ 150/-

8963 B • ₹ 80/-

8890 D • ₹ 150/-

9925 A • ₹ 60/-

For buying online visit our *website:* www.pustakmahal.com • *Email:* orders@pustakmahal.com

ALTERNATIVE THERAPIES

8882 F • ₹ 180/-

8983 E • ₹ 100/-

8836 D • ₹ 135/-

9935 F • ₹ 120/-

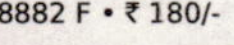

5637 D • ₹ 96/-

8889 D • ₹ 80/-

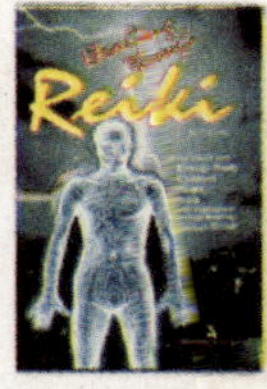

8842 D • ₹ 100/-

8941 A • ₹ 80/-

GENERAL HEALTH

9075 C • ₹ 225/-

8877 A • ₹ 120/-

9940 D • ₹ 150/-

8859 G • ₹ 80/-

9038 A • ₹ 68/-

8847 M • ₹ 100/-

8870 D • ₹ 100/-

9950 B • ₹ 120/-

9902 F • ₹ 120/-

COMMON AILMENTS & DISEASES

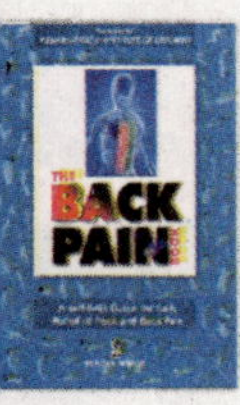

8891 D • ₹ 120/-

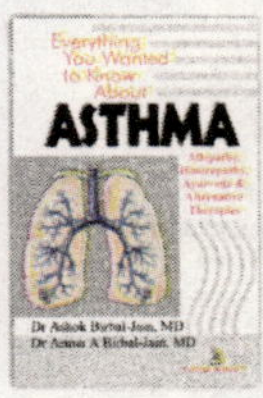

8281 A • ₹ 100/-

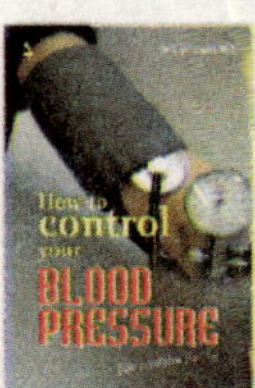

8094 D • ₹ 120/-

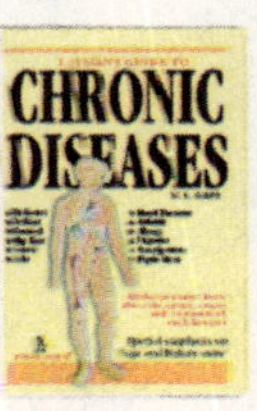

8848 D • ₹ 96/-

8276 A • ₹ 96/-

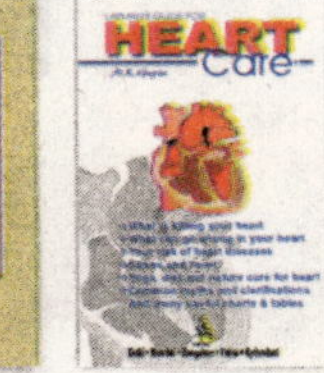

8888 D • ₹ 96/-

8908 D • ₹ 120/-

8878 B • ₹ 80/-

SLIMMING & FITNESS

8277 B • ₹ 120/-

8875 K • ₹ 120/-

9445 A • ₹ 150/-

DIET & NUTRITION

9941 D • ₹ 100/-

8904 D • ₹ 100/-

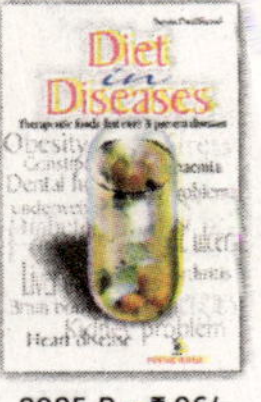

8985 B • ₹ 96/-

8968 G • ₹ 96/-

8271 C • ₹ 96/-

9037 D • ₹ 150/-

HINDOOLOGY / RELIGION / SPIRITUAL BOOKS

New

9873 C • ₹ 60/-

9770 E • ₹ 150/-

9799 D • ₹ 160/-

9453 A • ₹ 195/-

4179 A • ₹ 295/- (HB)

4128 D • ₹ 295/- (HB)

4138 B Rs. 250 (PB)

4181 C • ₹ 195/-

4177 B • ₹ 195/-

9997 C • ₹ 80/-

4182 D • ₹ 96/-

9984 E • ₹ 399/- (HB)

4130 B • ₹ 120/-

4183 A • ₹ 350/- (HB)

4151 A • ₹ 399/- (HB)

9811 P • ₹ 120/-

9585 A • ₹ 96/-

9405 A • ₹ 195/-

9989 D • ₹ 96/-

9508 D • ₹ 95/-

4134 B • ₹ 80/-

4188 A • ₹ 160/-

9504 D • ₹ 100/-

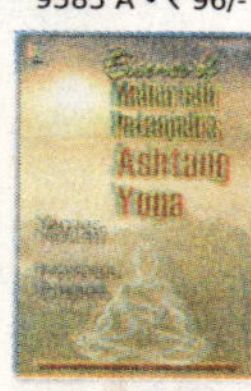

4133 A • ₹ 60/-

9513 A • ₹ 195/-

4126 B • ₹ 96/-

9812 R • ₹ 120/-

4152 B • ₹ 96/-

4407 C • ₹ 195/-

9504 D • ₹ 100/-

4124 A • ₹ 120/-

9513 A • ₹ 175/-

9520 C • ₹ 120/-

9987 E • ₹ 150/-

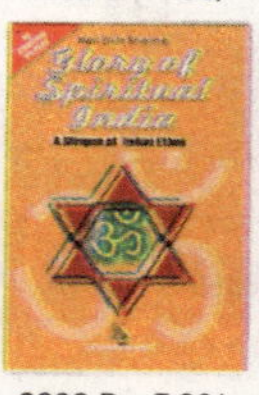

8898 D • ₹ 80/-

4190 C • ₹ 160/-

9509 A • ₹ 150/-

9510 B • ₹ 120/-

9525 A • ₹ 150/-

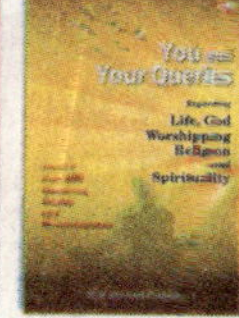

9540 D • ₹ 150/-

9542 B • ₹ 150/-

9514 B • ₹ 60/-

4132 D • ₹ 100/-

9069 A • ₹ 80/-

ASTROLOGY/VASTU/HYPNOTISM/PAMISTRY

FICTION

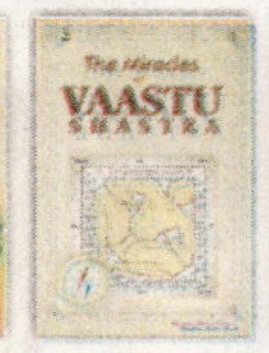

• ₹ 240/- 9693 H • ₹ 195/- 9671 F • ₹ 195/- 21_7 D • ₹ 150/- 4177 C • ₹ 195/- 9086 A • ₹ 295/-HB

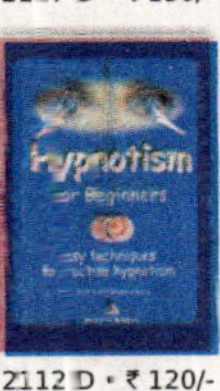

• ₹ 150/- 8259 D • ₹ 88/- 2109 F • ₹ 150/- 2112 D • ₹ 120/- 3110 B • ₹ 100/- 2133 B • ₹ 96/-

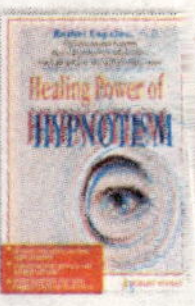

• ₹ 110/- 2125 D • ₹ 80/- 8925 D • ₹ 96/- 2132 A • ₹ 150/- 5432 D • ₹ 150/- 2120 D • ₹ 150/- 2109 F • ₹ 100/-

FIVE BOOKS

Set Price ₹ 495/- ₹ 99/- Each Volume

Set Code SH 001

THREE BOOKS

Set Price ₹ 297/- ₹ 99/- Each Volume

Set Code 9795 A

THREE BOOKS

Set Code 9752 B • ₹ 550/-

ENGLISH IMPROVEMENT

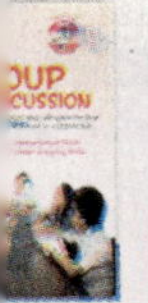

• ₹ 175/- 5541 C • ₹ 196/- 6651 E • ₹ 175/- 9448 D • ₹ _75/- 9056 A • ₹ 125/- 5538 D • ₹ 100/-

PARENTING

9906 J • ₹ 175/- (HB) 8261 D • ₹ 180/-

9674 J • ₹ 220/- 9784 J • ₹ 150/-

9594 K • ₹ 80/- 8917 D • ₹ 120/-

PERSON & PERSONALITIES

• ₹ 120/- 9825 E • ₹ 150/- 2113 D • ₹ 195/- 9764 R • ₹ 100/- 891_ D • ₹ 120/-

JOKES HUMOUR & SATIRE

2342 C • ₹ 100/- 2343 D • ₹ 100/-

2341 B • ₹ 60/- 2318 A • ₹ 96/-

2330 B • ₹ 96/- 2319 B • ₹ 96/-

BODY/BEAUTY CARE

• ₹ 150/- 9986 B • ₹ 150/- 8971 B • ₹ 120/- 9922 F • ₹ 120/- 8865 F • ₹ 120/-

FUN, FACTS, MAGIC & MYSTERIES

9484 B • ₹ 150/- 2275 D • ₹ 120/- 9479 M • ₹. 120/- 9470 B • ₹ 100/-

2208 M • ₹ 100/- 9816 D • ₹ 100/- 2247 F • ₹ 100/- 2250 A • ₹ 110/-

2211 F • ₹ 100/- 9457 E • ₹ 150/- 2237 M • ₹ 80/- 2335 A • ₹ 80/-

2243 L • ₹ 100/- 9775 M • ₹ 100/- 9985 A • ₹ 80/- 5110 A • ₹ 80/-

2337 C • ₹ 96/- 2336 B • ₹ 100/- 2331 C • ₹ 100/- 9977 B • ₹ 100/-

YOGA & MEDITATION

8269 A • ₹ 195/- 9998 D • ₹ 150/- 8939 D • ₹ 96/- 9080 C • ₹ [illegible]

with CD

9958 S • ₹ 160/- 9087 B • ₹ 150/- 2118 F • ₹ 120/-

8901 D • ₹ 150/- 8099 D • ₹ 80/- 9025 D • ₹ 80/-

HOMEOPATHY, AYURDEDA

9445 B • ₹ 150/- 8887 D • ₹ 195/- 8270 B • ₹ 195/- 8923 D • ₹ [illegible]

8010 D • ₹ 96/- 9094 E • ₹ 96/- 8944 D • ₹ 175/- 8948 A • ₹ [illegible]

WORLD FAMOUS SERIES

9472 D • ₹ 100/- 2337 C • ₹ 100/- 9483 A • Rs. 100/- 51107 • ₹ 100/- 9766 A • Rs. 100/- 9489 G • Rs. 100/- 9761 M • ₹ 120/-

World Famous Mysterious Objects
True Stories of Mowglis and other Wild Childrens
World Famous Treasures (Lost and Found)
World Famous WARs & Battles
True Stories of Mystic Places
World Famous Adventures
World Famous Military Operations
World Famous Spy Scandals
World Famous Spies & Spymasters
World Famous Crooks & Con Men
True Stories 81 Weird Humans
True Stories of Great Explorers
World Famous Ghosts
World Famous Strange Mysteries
and many more.......

₹ 100/- each boo[k]

LOVE, ROMANCE & SEX

9602 B • Rs. 125/- 8260 D • Rs. 96/- 8266 D • Rs. 80/- 8278 C • Rs. 100/- 8916 D • Rs. 120/-

MORAL, WISDOM & FAIRY TALES

9677 P • Rs. 150/- 9486 D • Rs. 250/- 9763 P • Rs. 150/- 8967 F • Rs. 80/- 9077 E • Rs.120/- 9563 N • R[illegible]